More praise for *How We Lead Matters*

"By turns humorous and heartfelt, this candid collection of snapshots by Marilyn offers valuable insights for anyone running a business or running a household."

—JAMES DIMON, CHAIRMAN & CHIEF EXECUTIVE OFFICER, JPMORGAN CHASE & CO.

"Whether through the words of a famous poet or her own, Marilyn's stories are powerful life lessons that will benefit any and all. Her accomplishments and personal reflections are an inspiration."

—BRENDA C. BARNES, CHAIRMAN AND CEO, SARA LEE CORPORATION

"My friend Tom Tewell says there are two 'most important days' in your life: the day you are born, and the day you understand why. Marilyn Carlson Nelson's life is a tribute to the 'why.'"

—BONNIE MCELVEEN-HUNTER, CHAIRMAN OF THE AMERICAN RED CROSS

"A poignant, heartfelt lesson on being a leader, and doing it with humanity and compassion. Marilyn brings forward the dilemmas many of us have or will face and with humility gives us her path on overcoming our own human foibles. It is brilliant, warm, and caring—a must read."

—ALAN G. HASSENFELD, CHAIRMAN, HASBRO

"With this one inspiring book, Marilyn has done more than 'level' the field for women. She guides us to higher ground, with her own extraordinary accomplishments modeling the change we as women want to see and to be as leaders."

—PAT MITCHELL, PRESIDENT & CEO, THE PALEY CENTER FOR MEDIA

"*How We Lead Matters* is a warm but clarion call for strong corporate leadership built on trust, discipline, transparency and commitment."

—CHARLES MOORE, EXECUTIVE DIRECTOR,
COMMITTEE ENCOURAGING CORPORATE PHILANTHROPY

"Marilyn's reflections on leadership are as thought provoking and practical as they are timeless. This book matters to all who have carried the responsiblity of leadership and anyone who aspires to attain it."

—TAMI LONGABERGER, CHIEF EXECUTIVE OFFICER AND
PRESIDENT OF THE LONGABERGER COMPANY

"Marilyn offers an insightful and candid account of the experiences she gained and the decisions she made both in her dining room and in the board room."

—JAY S. FISHMAN, CHAIRMAN AND CEO, THE TRAVELERS COMPANIES, INC.

"In her elegantly understated way, Marilyn offers shimmering pearls of wisdom about life, leadership, ambition, balance and, oh yes, rollerblading."

—Hugh Price, Former President, National Urban League
and Senior Fellow, Brookings Institution

"Finally! A book on leadership that you actually want to read! Marilyn is an exceptional storyteller, as well as a charismatic leader and one with integrity. It is inspirational and very motivating to learn from her experiences."

—Marsha Firestone, PhD, President and Founder, Women Presidents' Organization

"With considerable precision, grace, and economy Marilyn Carlson Nelson shows us that great leaders are formed from many small moments. You'll find yourself in many of her stories, and end up mining your own experience for such gold as well."

—Marc Benioff, Chairman & CEO, salesforce.com and author of The Business of
Changing the World: Twenty Great Leaders on Strategic Corporate Philanthropy

"Marilyn Carlson Nelson is a born leader, a trait I've always valued in the locker room and on the field. After reading these inspiring stories, I would have named Marilyn captain of all my football teams!"

—Lou Holtz, legendary coach and member of the College Football Hall of Fame

"Marilyn's stories are wonderfully witty, deeply authentic and inspiring for the rest of us. A must read for anyone navigating the journey to leadership."

—Beth A. Brooke, Global Vice Chair, Strategy &
Regulatory Affairs, Ernst & Young LLP

"There are snapshots of love, leadership, trauma, mentorship, and entrepreneurial dynamism. Marilyn has written a best seller that every man and woman should experience!"

—Terry Neese, CEO/President, Institute for Economic Empowerment of Women

"Choosing to lead matters, but the quality of leadership matters even more. Marilyn has given us a treasury of inspirational reflections on leadership based on her experiences as a wife, mother and grandmother, corporate CEO and engaged citizen."

—Melanne Verveer, Co-founder and Chairman, Vital Voices Global Partnership

"A unique combination of wisdom and wit to convey important lessons of life and leadership. . . . I highly recommend this entertaining read."

—Ann Veneman, Executive Director of UNICEF

How We Lead Matters
Reflections on a Life of Leadership

Marilyn Carlson Nelson

with

Deborah Cundy

Mc
Graw
Hill

New York   Chicago   San Francisco   Lisbon   London
Madrid   Mexico City   Milan   New Delhi   San Juan
Seoul   Singapore   Sydney   Toronto

The *McGraw-Hill* Companies

2 3 4 5 6 7 8 9 0   DOC/DOC   0 9 8

ISBN   978-0-07-160017-0
MHID   0-07-160017-5

Printed and bound by RR Donnelley.
McGraw-Hill books are available at special quantity discounts to use as premiums and sales promotions, or for use in corporate training programs. To contact a representative please visit the Contact Us pages at www.mhprofessional.com.

"I Live My Life in Growing Orbits" from SELECTED POEMS OF RAINER MARIA RILKE, A TRANSLATION FROM THE GERMAN AND COMMENTARY by ROBERT BLY. Copyright © 1981 Robert Bly. Reprinted by permission of HarperCollins Publishers.

From *Haiku Humor*, by Stephen Addiss, Fumiko Yamamoto, and Akira Yamamoto, © 2007 by Stephen Addiss, Fumiko Yamamoto, and Akira Yamamoto. Reprinted by arrangement with Shambhala Publications Inc., Boston, MA. www.shambhala.com.

"WHAT I KNOW NOW: Letter to My Younger Self" by Marilyn Carlson Nelson originally appeared in *What I Know Now*, edited by Ellyn Spragins and is reprinted with permission of Random House, Inc.

This book is printed on acid-free paper.

For

my husband, Glen;

my parents, Curt & Arleen;

my children, Diana, Curtis, Juliet, and Wendy;

my grandchildren, Alexander, Juliet, Jamie, Jenny, Martin, and Sadie

for teaching me what love is all about: romantic, gentle, tough, forgiving,

healing, sustaining, and lasting

Contents

Foreword

"Do not go where the path may lead," urged Ralph Waldo Emerson. "Go instead where there is no path . . . and leave a trail." Few have lived up to that message with more passion for a life of leadership than the woman who has given us these thoughtful and charming reflections on life.

Who better than Marilyn Carlson Nelson to be offered an invitation from the U.S. Air Force Thunderbirds to become the first "female CEO" to fly in an F-16 jet? There she went, blazing yet another trail. It was a memorable beginning to her decade-long tenure as CEO of Carlson—a decade now being celebrated as "The Super Decade."

Who else but Marilyn would show up for her first annual company meeting as CEO on rollerblades, with the entrance line, "Here we go, go, go, go!" There has never been anything presumptuous about her even as she is showered with honors and accolades for the way she has built Carlson into one of the largest travel, hospitality, and marketing companies in the world.

Who else but Marilyn could inspire us all by sharing the tragic story of her family's loss? Just days after dropping her daughter Juliet off at Smith College to begin her undergraduate studies, the call came that Juliet had been killed in an auto accident. During a prolonged period of grieving, Marilyn found solace in a speech that her daughter had given to her senior class just months before. She shares passages from that speech here as Juliet reminds her classmates (and us) that, "Life is always fragile . . . each one of us is given only one journey." Her mother took those thoughts to heart and has lived each day since to its fullest.

And finally, who else but Marilyn would have the persistence to follow her career dreams even in the face of naysayers? She tells the story of how one employer asked her to sign her reports with her initials, "M.C. Nelson" because he didn't believe anyone would take financial advice from a woman. Yet she persevered.

One of two daughters born to the ultra-entrepreneur, Curtis L. Carlson, Marilyn has often said that there weren't many silver spoons around in those early days of the family business. Family vacations were rare and if they ate out, dessert was forbidden—better to put the money back into the company. And as time went on, another point of view her father shared very publicly was his severe disappointment that he didn't have a son to whom he could entrust the business.

In the meantime, Marilyn raised her family, accepted community leadership roles and, when encouraged by outsiders, pondered a move into politics. It wasn't easy to win her father's approval, but after working in several positions within the family business, eventually he had to acknowledge she was the right leader at the right time.

To say that as an incoming CEO she inherited a booming success is to misunderstand just how significant her own contribution has been in the decade since. Harvard professor Bill George, a long-time friend of Marilyn's and the former CEO and Chair of Medtronic, has written: "When she took over Carlson . . . Marilyn inherited a demoralized organization suffering from decades of top-down rule. She immediately set about changing things, expressing empathy for her employees and compassion for her customers. The result: a remarkable turnaround with record levels of growth and new heights in employee and customer satisfaction."

Under her leadership, Carlson has turned into a global powerhouse. From a system-wide revenue base of $22 billion when she took over, it enjoyed revenues in 2007 of nearly $40 billion. Moreover, Marilyn made good on her promise to transform the corporate culture. Women now compose nearly 40 percent of executives.

Along the way, Marilyn has herself become a global powerhouse. A national selection committee organized by the Center for Public Leadership at Harvard's Kennedy School—a committee that I co-chaired with Warren Bennis—in 2006 voted to name her one of "America's Best Leaders" in a *U.S. News & World Report* survey. *Forbes* named her one of the "World's Most Powerful Women." President Bill Clinton appointed her as a leader at a White House Conference on Tourism, and after her highly successful efforts to revive the international tourism industry in the wake of September 11th, President Bush asked her to chair the National Women's Business Council. She has been a star at the World Economic Forum in

Davos, Switzerland, and was only the second woman to serve as co-chair of the forum's annual session.

Anyone who has had the privilege of hearing Marilyn's speeches knows that she often inserts a personal story . . . stories you aren't used to hearing from a CEO. Stories about how she nearly flunked an assignment in college economics, how she "fixed" her Sunday school class, how she won over the Super Bowl committee and how she has navigated the travails of motherhood including an invasion of gerbils. But the unifying, underlying message in all her speeches is: How we lead matters. And as you'll see in the stories in this book, she is a passionate champion of people at all levels, one who encourages others to step forward and lead. It comes as no surprise, therefore, that she is deeply involved in the development of our future leaders.

In 2007, it was my privilege to participate in the launch of the Center for Integrative Leadership at the University of Minnesota which Marilyn helped found. It was her vision and leadership which inspired the teaching and research needed to develop a new kind of leader for the 21st century: leaders who can work effectively across the public and private sectors to find new solutions to complex, societal problems; leaders who can connect the dots. As she says, "Some look at the sky and see just stars, but others see patterns. 'Look, there's a hunter, there's a goddess, isn't that a bear?' And, we'll never see the sky in the same way again."

As they look back, many business and political leaders write long, ponderous memoirs recounting every title and milestone of their careers while masking their inner feelings. Thankfully, Marilyn has given us just the opposite. Here, in these brief remembrances, she reveals who she is at her core, what she treasures, and how her values have guided her on her journey. She wrote this, as she says, so that her grandchildren could know her more fully. But it deserves a much wider audience because it contains timeless wisdom for others as they make their own journey, hoping to leave a trail.

When I think of Marilyn—and I have been privileged to know her as a friend for several years—she always strikes me as the walking embodiment of the credo that she has so energetically promoted at Carlson:

Whatever you do, do with Integrity
Wherever you go, go as a Leader
Whomever you serve, serve with Caring
Whenever you dream, dream with your All
And never, ever give up.

That's Marilyn—right down to the rollerblades!

DAVID GERGEN
Professor of Public Service
Director, Harvard Kennedy School's
Center for Public Leadership

Author's Acknowledgment

This book is a collection of remembrances of people and times in my life from which I've learned lessons that may provide some insight or guidance to others. There are many, many more people who have enriched my life and supported my leadership than I could possibly mention within these pages. I wish to express my gratitude to:

Deborah Cundy and Doug Cody, who have covered thousands of miles with me on my spiritual and intellectual journey as well as my professional one, helping me express my vision, my values and—my vulnerabilities. To Deb, for encouraging me to finish what we started a couple years earlier when we first developed the concept for this book, and to Doug, Carlson's vice president–executive communications, for collaborating with me on my speeches, many of which have included these stories.

My sister, Barby, and her husband, Skip Gage, their children and grandchildren as well as our aunts, uncles and cousins—all 80 of them—with whom we share every Christmas and Fourth of July.

Hennepin Avenue United Methodist Church and its ministries, from Robert Raines and Chester Pennington to David Scoates and Bruce Robbins each of whom has baptized, married and/or buried our various family members for 75 years and who have taught me of unconditional divine love.

Trudy Rautio, Bill Van Brunt, Jeff Balagna, Jim Porter and Kim Olson—executives of Carlson and more than colleagues, who have bonded as family.

Curtis Nelson, Jay Witzel, Richard Snead, Mark Conroy, Michael Batt, Jim Schroer, Hubert Joly, Paul Kirwin, Kurt Ritter, Jasminder Singh, Boris Ivesha, Herve Gourio and John Norlander who have successfully led our businesses to global positions.

Mark Herreid, John Flottmeier, Matt Van Slooten, and, before them, Dean Riesen for guiding our family office and real estate company.

Beth Rosenbloom, Bev McGinty and Faye Allen in my office for their daily, nightly (and sometimes weekend) support and cherished friendship.

Bob Dilenschneider for his wise counsel and suggestion that I do "something with my love for poetry" which inspired this book.

My dear friends, especially Sue Hodder, Luella Goldberg, Barbara Burwell, Karen Baker, Sherry Davis, Harvey Mackay, Ken Dayton, Ron Lund, and Paul Ridgeway who made thousands of volunteer hours truly joyful, rewarding experiences in my life.

Dick Cisek and Jim Colville who, as leaders of the Minnesota Orchestra and United Way, gave me responsibility before I had earned it.

Harry Holtz, Don Grangaard, Jack MacAllister, Larry Rawls, Lee Raymond, Rex Tillerson, Win Wallin, Denis Cortese—CEOs of board of directors on which I have served—for their models of values-based leadership.

Her Majesty Queen Silvia of Sweden, Klaus Schwab, Phillip Brunelle, Neville Marriner, Osmo Vanska, Bill George, David Gergen, Peter Brabeck and Nick Bollettieri for inspiring me by word and deed to use every platform possible to improve the human condition.

Nelson Mandela, Desmond Tutu, U.S. Vice President Hubert Humphrey, France's Minister of Finance Christine Lagarde, President of Iceland Vigdis Finnbogadottir, President of Ireland Mary Robinson and Minnesota Governor Elmer Anderson who have taught me the true meaning of public servant.

Ron Brandt and Michael Hrupek for their creative contributions to the cover design and my patient and skillful editor at McGraw-Hill, Donya Dickerson, for guiding me through the book writing process my first time out.

To others I haven't mentioned, forgive me. I can never acknowledge my debt of gratitude for the experiences we have shared. God willing, I will have the time to tell more stories.

Introduction

I wandered lonely as a cloud
That floats on high o'er vales and hills,
When all at once I saw a crowd,
A host, of golden daffodils;
Beside the lake, beneath the trees,
Fluttering and dancing in the breeze. . . .

For oft, when on my couch I lie
In vacant or in pensive mood,
They flash upon that inward eye
Which is the bliss of solitude;
And then my heart with pleasure fills,
And dances with the daffodils.

WILLIAM WORDSWORTH
(BRITISH POET)
FROM "I WANDERED LONELY AS A CLOUD"

On a recent visit to Minnesota from his home in California, my 13-year-old grandson, Jamie, startled me. "Were you alive during segregation?" he asked.

In that moment, I realized that although we had shared meaningful moments since his birth—from baptism to homework, family vacations, soccer and hockey, not to mention virtually every holiday—he didn't know me.

In speeches I have delivered all over the world as a global CEO, I have told stories of formative moments in my life and career. I have revealed humorous anecdotes in which the joke's on me. I've shared treasured memories of Carlson colleagues, and I've often repeated the wise words of the corporate and world leaders I have had the privilege of knowing. Somehow, in the haste of life, these reflections weren't being shared with some of the most important people in my life.

One day, there will be a definitive history of Carlson, detailing the growth of the Carlson brands: Radisson and Regent hotels and resorts, Country Inns & Suites By Carlson, Park Inn and Park Plaza hotels, Regent Seven Seas Cruises, Carlson Wagonlit Travel, Carlson Marketing, and T.G.I. Friday's restaurants. Carlson often has been described as one of the most successful private companies in the United States for its longevity and global reach. It certainly has provided me with great personal satisfaction to have participated in its success for more than twenty years, the last ten as CEO.

The short stories contained within these pages are the ones that are closest to me. They have stayed in my memory—surviving the successive waves of the years—like the relics of a sand castle in the morning. They survive, I guess, because they tell my truths.

So although I started out to compile these remembrances for my grandchildren, I have come to realize that these stories, accompanied by a few favorite poems and quotes, reveal the core principles and beliefs that have guided my life and career. And they have served me well.

I hope that you will enjoy them for what they are: not the grand expounding of a corporate leader but the lessons learned from the everyday experiences of a mother, wife, and grandmother who happens to be a CEO. Perhaps they will inspire you to take a moment to let those who are to follow know you. Perhaps you will remind them that life is made up of a series of days and choices and that how we lead matters.

MARILYN CARLSON NELSON
THANKSGIVING 2007

How We Lead Matters
Reflections on a Life of Leadership

Knowledge of how to combine
is the mother of all
other forms of knowledge.

ALEXIS DE TOCQUEVILLE
(FRENCH HISTORIAN)

Star Gazing

Business is one of the most powerful forces on the planet—for good or for ill. Its domain is far-reaching and pervasive. Those of us who are "called to business" as our life pursuit must learn how best to leverage our influence and work across sectors on complex problems for the common good. We must be what I call "integrative leaders."

I am reminded of the story of Ruth Shaw, the first woman to head a U.S. power company. When she was tapped for the top job, she was baffled. She knew she didn't have a deep specialization in a particular competency such as marketing, human resources, business law, or operations. The chairman told her, "I have accountants, lawyers, and salespeople. I need someone who can connect the dots." We know that connecting the dots within a company is critical to success. But connecting the dots *between* a company and the outside world may be as important to the world as it is to the company.

Do you think, for example, in August 2001, I had any idea that a small group of people living in caves in Afghanistan could bring my business to its knees? I did not. And then there was September 11. . . . Do you think that throughout my education I ever thought it might be useful to take a course in engineering? I did not. And then there was Six Sigma. . . . Do you think I could imagine the need to give speeches in defense of business as a morally upstanding way to earn a living? I did not. And then there was Enron.

In an increasingly complex and interconnected world, business leaders must pause and contemplate the way our businesses can best interact with the nonprofit and public sectors. It's not unlike the way the ancients looked at the skies: some just saw stars, but others saw the patterns of dogs, bears, goddesses, and hunters. They connected the dots, and we'll never again see the sky in the same way.

Never doubt that a small group of thoughtful,
committed citizens can change the world.
Indeed, it's the only thing that ever has.

MARGARET MEAD

(U.S. ANTHROPOLOGIST)

The Sunday School Lesson

Of all the gifts given to me by my father, the greatest was personal responsibility.

Our family always went to church on Sunday, and because I was in the seventh grade, I attended Sunday school classes instead of the main service. One day, after a particularly chaotic class with flying spitballs and little or no order, I announced to my parents on the ride home that I was quitting Sunday school and from then on would be going to the main sanctuary with the adults.

Instead of praising my maturity, as I thought he would, my dad pulled off the highway, turned around, and said, "You *what?*" When I repeated my complaint that Sunday school was of little value, he looked at me sternly and said, "Then change it." Keep in mind that I was only 13 and my father was ordering me to fix a Sunday school that even the adult teachers couldn't control!

My mother tried to intercede and for her trouble was given the job of setting up a meeting with the Sunday school superintendent so that I could present my ideas for fixing things. When the day came, she drove me downtown to the big meeting. I was nervous, to say the least. But the superintendent was pleased to hear my ideas, and together we "fixed" Sunday school.

From that early lesson I learned that if something needs to change in our homes, schools, workplaces, or churches, it's up to us to change it rather than wait for "they" or "them" or someone else to do it.

Everyone is entitled to their own opinions,
but not their own facts.

DANIEL P. MOYNIHAN
(U.S. SENATOR)

As a Matter of Fact

Part of my college career was spent studying international economics and political science at the Institute des Hautes Etudes Economiques et Politiques in Geneva, Switzerland. Away from home in that stimulating setting, I was filled with confidence and idealism.

I learned a great deal that year, but one lesson in particular has served me well throughout my business career.

One day, my professor asked a classmate and me to debate two sides of an economic philosophy in front of a very large audience and in French, no less. I painstakingly translated my points and rehearsed until I could recite my side of the argument fluently. On the day of the debate, I laid out a compelling case, illuminated by my personal belief.

At the end of my energetic and colorful presentation, the audience applauded wildly. I felt supremely victorious and certain of my success—until I received my grade. It was the worst grade I'd ever received.

Perplexed, I confronted the professor. "I don't understand," I said. "My argument was a huge success. You were there. The audience loved it."

"Yes, Marilyn, your performance was brilliant," he conceded. "But your facts must equal your passion."

Even the winner
of the argument
has a hard time sleeping

TAKASHIMA GYOKUTORO
(JAPANESE POET)

Payback

In my second year at Smith College, I agreed to arrange a mixer at a down-town ballroom on behalf of my class. The tradition at the time was for the girls to submit the names of boys they knew who were going to schools in the area. The boys wouldn't know which girl invited them, as the invitation went out from the "Sophomore Class of Smith." When the RSVPs started coming in, we realized our boy–girl ratio was falling short.

In the second round of invitations, I remembered the name of a hand-some Harvard pre-med student, Glen Nelson, who was from my hometown of Edina, Minnesota. A couple days later, Glen called me, insisting that I had submitted his name. I denied it. (What nerve!) Anyway, who cared? (Besides the two of us, that is.) Glen accepted the invitation. And to punctuate my indifference, I told him to bring a couple of other guys to fill in.

He showed up an hour and a half early with two cars full of star athletes and announced that they were all there for dinner. I still don't know if I was more furious that my hair was uncombed and I wasn't dressed for the event or that, as the hostess, I was responsible for paying per head.

I stormed upstairs and announced to my classmates that guests were starting to arrive, and by the way, I wouldn't be joining them for dinner. There was a stunned silence. When I got to the part in my rant about who *would* be at dinner, I lost every sympathetic ear. The requests came in a flurry about who wanted to sit next to which athlete.

I heard that the dinner was lovely. Some new relationships bloomed. How nice. Every place was taken. I know; I paid the bill. And in the end, I eventually did get even with Glen Nelson. I married him.

Marilyn Carlson Nelson

It's never too late to be
what you might have been.

GEORGE ELIOT
(BRITISH NOVELIST)

Wanting It All

WHAT I KNOW NOW: *Letters to My Younger Self* is a unique book of advice letters from successful women such as Maya Angelou, Madeleine Albright, and Queen Noor written to their "younger selves." Here's an excerpt from mine:

Dear Marilyn:

You have ambitious dreams that seem to include every possibility under the sun. You want to be a mother. You want exactly four children. You also want to be a political leader or diplomat. You want to serve as a community leader and you want one day to have a meaningful role in your family's business at Carlson.

Those who know you wonder why you think you can do it all. How can you possibly reconcile all those dreams into one lifetime? Maybe you should let some go. What I know now is that women can actually come pretty close to having it all, but you just can't have it all every day.

If you look at each stage of your life as an opportunity to [make a difference], your effectiveness will increase, your reputation will grow and extraordinary possibilities will present themselves. In the end, you weren't really dreaming about titles or position or even about being a wife or mother. Rather, you were dreaming about living the life that would complete you.

Let it unfold,

Marilyn

(from *WHAT I KNOW NOW* Ellyn Spragins)

In the depth of winter,
I finally learned that there was
within me an invincible summer.

ALBERT CAMUS
(FRENCH NOVELIST AND PHILOSOPHER)

The Signature

There was a time in my life when I truly did not know how I could carry on.

The sunshine had been abruptly eclipsed by the call telling me our daughter, Juliet, had been killed in an automobile accident while preparing to attend her first year of classes at Smith College. Smith was my alma mater, where I had left my daughter weeks before with all the promise of a young life ahead of her. And then the call came.

Like most who have lost a loved one unexpectedly, I cycled through feelings of pain and anger that ultimately led to abject depression. Though I was surrounded by a loving family trying to help, nothing seemed to reach me.

My faith was sorely tested. How could God let this happen? I finally rejected God and read every philosopher I could find, trying to understand.

Eventually, with my faith renewed, my husband and I realized that we could best remember our daughter by making a new commitment to living our lives to the fullest. Because it may be our last, we must live each day in a way that we would be proud to "sign our name" to it, just as an artist signs his or her work with pride of accomplishment.

From that day, we have devoted ourselves to making each day count— to living the rich, full life that was denied our Juliet.

Marilyn Carlson Nelson

O wad some Power the giftie gie us,
To see oursels as ithers see us!

ROBERT BURNS
(SCOTTISH POET)

The Times They Are A-Changin'

The Great Depression had a deep and lasting impact on my father, as it did on most of his generation. When he became a successful entrepreneur in the 1970s and 1980s, he still carried with him the life experiences of his time. He valued capital above all. Understandably so—in the 1930s, money was scarce but employees were plentiful.

I'll never forget the day in the early 1990s when we paid a visit together to a class of MBA students at the Carlson School of Management at the University of Minnesota.

At one point, with much hubris, my father asked if the students were planning to apply for jobs at Carlson. There was a long silence.

One of them finally spoke up and said, "No." Incredulous, my father asked why. The student replied that he had heard that Carlson had a reputation for not valuing its employees. My father went white. It was a brutal reality.

Jobs in today's environment depend much more on brains than brawn. The competition for talent can be fierce. On the surface it sounds simple: My company sells hotel rooms, restaurant meals, and tickets on airplanes. But I am really in the business of hiring the most talented people I can find to ensure a differentiated experience for our customers. I am in a talent war.

In that classroom, I felt somewhat sorry for my very proud father, who didn't understand that the rules had changed. But who does when you've been playing the game so brilliantly for so long?

Some cause happiness wherever they go;
others whenever they go.

OSCAR WILDE
(BRITISH AUTHOR)

Laughter as Legacy

I was young and fearless and, truth be told, a bit arrogant when I announced to the legendary comedian, Danny Kaye, that I had come to audition him for a charity event for the Minnesota Orchestra.

"So, you're here to audition me?" he said with a boyish smile. "I don't think I've been auditioned in 40 years. Have a seat." I sat down at his kitchen table with his manager of three decades, Herb Bonice. My idea was for Danny to conduct the "Tivoli Ball" as the Hans Christian Andersen character he had portrayed in the 1952 classic film.

"Well, let's see," he said thoughtfully. "I might consider doing this. But I have some conditions." I opened my notebook, ready to accommodate.

"I need South African resin for the floor. What kind do they use in Minnesota?" "I don't know," I said earnestly, "but I'll find out."

"And carnations. These have always been good luck for me. They should be red," he said. "Oh, and there needs to be 137 of them . . . exactly." I scribbled each word in my notebook.

"And wooden hangers. I can't stand those slippery metal ones." By then I was considering retracting my offer, but I noticed a glint in Herb's eye. I slammed my book shut and threw down my pen. "Now you've gone too far!" We all collapsed in childish glee.

After his death, I read that a priest said of Danny Kaye, "Any fool can be solemn, but only a saintly person can be a fool."

Amen.

Oh, yes, he did conduct the Minnesota Orchestra.

He drew a circle that shut me out
Heretic, rebel, a thing to flout
But love and I had the wit to win—
We drew a circle that took him in.

EDWIN MARKHAM
(U.S. POET)

Imagine

Sometimes I engage in a simple mental game. My college minor in theater helps me, but I believe it's a game everyone can—and should—play once in a while. You could call the game "Can You Imagine?"

The goal is to try to imagine how another person felt in a certain situation. It's a step beyond empathy, really. It's more like closing your eyes and becoming that person—hearing what that person heard, feeling what he or she felt.

Try it: Imagine that you are a 6 year-old girl, the year is 1960, you live in racially segregated New Orleans, Louisiana—and you are black. Because of a recent Supreme Court decision, you are going to your first day of school at an all-white grade school. Your name is Ruby Bridges. Can you imagine the terror that little Ruby felt walking into school between two rows of six-foot armed federal marshals?

Here's another: It's 1955, and you're a 37 year-old colored woman (in the parlance of the day) heading home on the bus from your job as a seamstress in Montgomery, Alabama.

You know the bus laws in Montgomery: You must pay your fare to the driver, get off, and re-board through the back door. You must sit in the back, in the "colored section." If the white section is full and another white passenger gets on, you must give up your seat and move farther to the back.

On this day, you find a seat, but then the bus begins to fill up. Soon the bus driver approaches and tells you to give up your seat to a white passenger. You refuse. He says that if you don't, he will have you arrested.

You reply: "You may go on and do so." Can you imagine?

How wonderful it is that nobody
need wait a single moment
before starting to improve the world.

When I Grow Up

She ran to the car, one knee sock around her ankle, her barrette askew in her hair. She barely had opened the car door when she announced with a big smile that she had written an "essay." It obviously had been a good day in fourth grade for my oldest daughter, Diana.

"Good for you, sweetheart!" I thought it was important that I respond with the same enthusiasm. "What did you choose to write about in your essay?"

"Well," she said very seriously, as if she were telling a secret. "It's about what I want to do when I grow up."

"I'm not sure you've ever shared that with me," I said. "What *do* you want to do?"

She pulled herself up very straight in her seat and said, "I want to make a difference."

It was Diana's voice, but I realized she was speaking for all of us who deep down inside yearn to leave our footprint. Maybe as we get older, we lose the courage to think it, say it—lest we fail.

But the truth is, we all want to be a part of something bigger. We all want to make a difference in some way, to someone.

Of course, ever since the day she was born, Diana has made a difference in my life. And as the years pass, I find myself turning often to her for a shoulder to lean on and wise counsel.

And the best part? We still share secrets.

Everyone has his own Atlantic to fly.
Whatever you want very much to do,
against the opposition of tradition,
neighborhood opinion and
so-called "common sense"—
that is an Atlantic.

AMELIA EARHART
(U.S. AVIATOR)

Flying Solo

Before I decided to join my father's business, or as he would remind me, before he *invited* me to join the business, I had hurdles to jump.

I initially worked part-time for the company in the communications area and, in my usual way, threw myself into the job, making it much more than part-time. At one point, my father decided that I couldn't possibly be paying enough attention to my four young children if I was spending all that time and energy on the company. One day, in a very brusque way, he sent me home. I cried all the way down the back steps.

Several years later, when my children were nearly grown and my husband was a busy surgeon, I was anxious to quicken my pace. It wasn't until I was being courted to run for governor of Minnesota that my potential—as perceived by others—got my father's attention and he asked me back. But exactly what kind of a career path I was entering into was not clear.

My father never hid the fact that he was disappointed that he did not have a son to step into his role. And until the day he announced in his eighty-third year that I would become CEO, I never assumed that I would. Like a horse frightened by the ever-increasing height of the bar, I often wanted to back away, afraid that I wouldn't make it. But I kept jumping.

Over the years, my father convinced himself that I could handle the job and often referred to me as "First Daughter, Only Son." One title inherited, one title bestowed. Thanks, Dad, for both.

What is done to children,
they will do to society.

DR. KARL MENNINGER
(U.S. PSYCHIATRIST)

Security Alarm

It is not commonly known, but slavery is not extinct. It continues to exist and is growing at record numbers in every corner of the world. Millions of people are entrapped in this atrocity, and sadly, much of this illicit activity involves children forced into prostitution. Officially, the number of children exploited in this way is reported to be two million at any given moment, but experts warn that that's just the tip of the iceberg.

Fortunately, there are many good people working to protect vulnerable children, most notably Her Majesty Queen Silvia of Sweden, at whose request Carlson was pleased to become a co-founder of the World Childhood Foundation, an organization that works to care for the world's street children and abandoned youth.

The sense of responsibility we must share for the world's children hit me like a thunderbolt many years ago as I was welcoming our newborn grandchild to our home for his first overnight visit.

I had prepared a nursery as any grandparent might, and entering it on the first morning of the visit, I felt an indescribable joy as I lifted him from the bed. It was a perfect moment: The sunlight even shone through the window, creating a glow around this perfect baby's head.

Suddenly I had a profound insight: This child is so loved by so many, yet all of our personal success and nurturing won't be able to protect him if we don't do something on behalf of those children in the world without a family, without hope, and without a future.

The truth is that there are no walls long enough or high enough to separate those we love from those who have known only abuse and pain.

Mettons en commun ce que nous
avons de meilleur et
enrichissons-nous de nos différences.

(Let us each put in common
the best that we have and
enrich ourselves with our differences.)

Paul Valéry
(French author and poet)

I Confess

I have a confession: I think I could have done more sooner to work for a level playing field for women in business. The truth is, I was so busy doing my job during most of my career, I just didn't focus a lot on the fact that I often was the only woman in the room.

When I was a securities analyst in the 1960s, I remember thinking how ridiculous it was that I was requested to sign my name with my initials "M.C. Nelson" because my employer didn't believe anyone would take financial advice from a woman. I also remember how elated I was to hear that I was getting my own office until I learned it was because I was pregnant and women in my "condition" needed to be out of sight. I suppose I could have railed against the injustices, but I enjoyed my work immensely and felt "grateful" to be doing what I loved.

Now, as CEO of a global company, I am more determined than ever to attract and retain the best and brightest candidates from the largest talent pool possible—one that includes both genders and certainly all races and ethnicities. The facts are in: diverse companies and teams consistently outperform all others. It's not only the smart thing and the right thing, it makes getting the job done much more interesting.

As we confront the most daunting challenges of our time, we need all the creativity, resolve, and leadership we can muster to find sustainable solutions in an increasingly complex world. Men and women must do it together. After all, if the village were on fire, would we expect only the men to help?

The louder he talked of his honor,
the faster we counted our spoons.

Ralph Waldo Emerson
(U.S. poet)

Gerbils for Sale

"We won!" shouted my youngest daughter, Wendy. What we "won" was the privilege of taking care of the third grade's gerbil family over the summer. We set them up in the laundry room, where they soon began giving birth. Within weeks, we had habitat trails running up and down the laundry room counter-tops. The day my favorite blouse came down the clothes chute—one sleeve falling into the gerbil pen and quickly being annihilated—was the day I knew I had to take action.

I called the pet store to inquire what might humanely be done. "Are you the gerbil lady?" the store clerk asked, explaining that they already had a preferred supplier. Armed with this insider information, I called the next pet store and identified myself as a gerbil supplier. (Well, in a sense I was.) It so happened they were low. When I arrived, the store manager commented that he thought my "crop" looked a little weak-eyed and asked if there had been inbreeding. But he'd take them at a reduced price. Afraid that he would back out of the deal if I gave them to him free, I . . . I . . . I took the money.

As heads of business, government, and even households, we are called upon to be successful *and* lawful *and* moral. It is a heavy burden, to be sure. There's always the danger that an action in the gray zone will result in a win that leads to the next incremental "creep" in judgment.

In my lifetime, I occasionally have wandered into the gray zone. I know I'm there whenever I sense that same uneasiness I felt in the pet store. I just hope I always draw the line at gerbils.

You must be the change
you want to see in the world.

MAHATMA GANDHI
(INDIAN NATIONALIST LEADER)

Power of One

My last visit to India reminded me of my first, 16 years earlier. I again was struck instantly by its vibrancy, its color, the warmth of its people—but at the same time overcome with a feeling of profound helplessness in the face of so much poverty, so many challenges. What difference could one person make?

Like many business leaders who visit India, I saw highly sophisticated call centers and technology companies where thousands of young people were building careers in industries that hadn't existed there a decade earlier. One by one, they were making a difference for themselves and their families in their new careers. I felt hopeful until I stepped back out into the street and again was confronted with so much need. What could one person do?

I would receive the answer to my question during my last night in New Delhi, at dinner with a woman who owned her own architectural firm. She was very engaged in taking on social issues in a country where the problems are so immense; many understandably would throw up their hands and say, "I just don't have enough resources to make a difference. Why bother?"

When I asked her how she carried on in the face of such abject need, she reminded me of the story of Gandhi. He had only five possessions: a cloth garment, a walking staff, a broken pair of eyeglasses, a pair of wooden sandals, and a pocket watch. Yet he transformed the world with his commitment and compassion.

Marilyn Carlson Nelson   *31*

The four oak walls of this chest were for thousands of miles to enclose and protect their essentials; to these planks would be entrusted most of their belongings . . . and the ancient clothes chest which was about to pass into an altogether new and eventful epoch of its history was given a new name in its old age. Through its new name it was set apart from all its equals and from all other belongings. It was called the "America chest."

VILHELM MOBERG

(SWEDISH AUTHOR)

FROM *THE EMIGRANTS*

Packing Light

When I learned that I was to be honored as Swedish American of the Year, I decided it would be the perfect opportunity to take my grandchildren to Sweden, where their ancestors on my father's side originated.

I quickly realized that the many formal dinners, long speeches, and late nights were quite trying for children. The discontent is well documented in one photo in which all the grandchildren have joined me on stage with King Carl Gustaf XVI and Queen Silvia. If you look closely, you'll see that 8 year-old Jenny is barefoot, having kicked off her shoes in boredom.

It seemed that at every expression of my enthusiasm, they questioned me about why they should be impressed with our Swedish ancestry since they were not just Swedish but also English, Welsh, Romanian, and Pakistani. I told them that the point is to find something in the culture that makes them proud of their ancestry—all of it. My suggestion was greeted by blank stares and silence. It definitely wasn't turning out to be the sentimental journey to our ancestral roots that I'd had in mind.

Alone at last at a family-only dinner on our final night, one of the grandchildren announced that they would put on a "show" of the trip. Amazingly, one by one they retraced our steps, quoting from my speeches about Sweden's accomplishments and telling our family's story.

"Each person packed a trunk," recited Jamie, describing the dilemma of distant ancestors, "The key is that they had to decide what to take with them: tools to shape their new world, mementos to remind them of where they came from, their faith to sustain them, and finally, they needed to know what to leave behind."

True of each generation no matter how far the journey.

Dancers are
the athletes of God.

ALBERT EINSTEIN
(GERMAN SCIENTIST)

The Dance

I ate very little for several days before my meeting with the choreographer Bob Jani. Bob had helped save Radio City Music Hall by "re-energizing" the Rockettes. Part of his strategy was to put them on a strict diet. I needed every advantage.

My goal was to persuade Bob to choreograph a United Way of Minneapolis halftime event at a Vikings football game. I thought I had an idea that could engage volunteers and the community more deeply in raising money for the city's growing needs. Bob politely pointed out that his fee would take a serious bite out of the campaign goal. Yes, but I explained that this was something he had never done before. He was skeptical.

"If you've done it," I said, "I'll consider us friends and go home. If you haven't done it, I'll ask that you give me a good price." He agreed.

"Have you ever choreographed wheelchairs?" I asked. He smiled. I knew we had a deal.

At halftime, a long, colorful line of wheelchairs entered the stadium. flanked by 2,000 volunteers. The group moved in perfect unison, creating beautifully shaped patterns to original music: "Love Makes the Difference." For the final movement, all the volunteers sequentially fell to their knees alongside the wheelchairs, forming a gigantic heart. The crowd was on its feet. The applause was thunderous.

From our places in the catbird seat high above the field, I turned to Bob to congratulate him on his success. "Look, Marilyn!" he said, his eyes filled with tears. "Everyone on the field has spontaneously joined hands at *exactly* the same moment. I never told them to do that."

If I am not for myself,
who will be for me?
If I am only for myself,
what am I?
And if not now,
when?

RABBI HILLEL THE ELDER
(JEWISH RELIGIOUS LEADER)

It's Time

Throughout the ages, the words of the great Talmudic sage Hillel have been echoed by many. We recall Robert F. Kennedy's exhortation: "If not now, when? If not us, who?"

How well I remember my own encounter with this age-old truth that right now is always the right time to do the right thing. It was years ago, at a time when I was serving on the board of Northwestern Bell.

This was during the breakup of AT&T into the "Baby Bells." Jack MacAllister was Northwestern Bell's CEO, and like most of his counterparts across the system, he was negotiating with AT&T about how his company should spin off and how resources and assets would be divided. It was a tense time.

In the middle of that ordeal, Jack came to a board meeting and said, "We've got a problem." He described how our women and minority managers—people we had trained, developed, and promoted—weren't being allowed to join the Rotary and Lion's Clubs in their communities. At the time, those clubs, where important networking took place and business was done, didn't accept women or minorities.

Jack informed the board that he was going to pull financial support from all those civic organizations throughout our service area. It would be wrong, he said, to support such discriminatory actions, especially against our own employees. Some board members cautioned him not to take this on at a time when the company was fighting through the breakup with AT&T.

This tall man with a quiet voice, angular face, and big hands—somewhat Lincoln-like, as I remember—simply looked at us and asked, "Oh? When *is* the time?"

There are two lasting bequests
we can give our children.
One is roots, the other wings.

HODDING CARTER III
(U.S. ASSISTANT SECRETARY OF STATE)

Open for Business

The carnivals in our backyard grew bigger by the year. Neighbors came from miles around to do the cakewalks, pull silly prizes from the fishpond, and buy a chance at the dunking machine to plunge my daughter, Wendy, and me into a tank of cold water. My son, Curtis, who orchestrated the annual event, was turning out to be quite the businessman.

I realized he had outgrown the carnival when one summer day he shocked me by coming down the stairs in a sport coat and announcing that he was off to city hall to get a variance to install a waterskiing course in front of our dock on the lake.

A couple of months later, I arrived home to find several dozen cars lining our driveway and parked on the lawn. All sorts of strangers in bathing suits, representing every stage of undress, were pulling waterski gear out of their cars.

I found Curtis in the middle of the activity down by the lake and asked what on earth was going on. He proudly announced that it was the "First International Stubbs Bay Waterskiing Contest," which, I came to find out, he had advertised in ski magazines.

"*What* are we going to do with all these people?" I asked.

"Well, if I were you, I'd sell hot dogs," he replied.

I learned something quite miraculous about motherhood that day. It is entirely possible to hold two opposing thoughts about your child at the same time. How I marveled at his ambition, and how I wanted to clock him.

Remember, you never
have to sing my songs.

A Super Sale

Frankly, selling snow to Eskimos would have been an easier assignment than trying to convince the Super Bowl committee that January in Minnesota had all the makings for a festive national get-together. When I accepted the Governor's invitation to chair the Super Bowl committee, I knew there was no predisposition whatsoever to bring the game north. They had tried that only once before—in Detroit—in a snowstorm.

We would have to pull out all the stops.

I went for a little humor. At a bidding committee meeting, when my competitors were asked about the mean January temperature in their cities, I knew I was in trouble. "78, 81, 68, 77. . . ." As my turn approached, I braced for the inevitable. I must have hesitated because the NFL official repeated the question, "*Mean* January temperature?"

I replied, "Yes." Laughter is a good deflector.

I resorted to a little exaggeration. When asked how many limos we had in the city, I counted the ones at the mortuaries. No matter if fans had to ride to the game lying down.

I threw in a little chocolate—always hard to resist. I personally dropped off life-size chocolate mallards at the NFL team owners' hotels and was known thereafter as the "The Duck Lady."

In 1992, Minnesota hosted the Super Bowl. The weather was on our side. We showed off our city beautifully. But perhaps most important to me, my father, who was considered an American icon of salesmanship, was there to enjoy my triumph. He sat beside me at the game, never once casting his shadow.

My candle burns at both ends;
It will not last the night;
But ah, my foes, and oh, my friends—
It gives a lovely light!

EDNA ST. VINCENT MILLAY
(U.S. POET)
"FIRST FIG"

Going for Gold

I often am asked, mostly by women, how to maintain a healthy work-life balance. I find that somewhat amusing because I don't have much of it. But I don't think many CEOs do—it comes with the territory. There is always one more phone call to make, one more memo to read, one more e-mail to send. And even in my leisure time, I am acutely aware that I am the CEO of a global company with nearly 160,000 employees and their families who depend on the company's well-being.

On good days, I am supremely satisfied with my choice. On bad days, I am quite certain that I've made a mistake at great personal cost. But all along, it has been *my* choice. I could have settled for less.

The fact is that being a leader in any field requires discipline, effort, and, yes, sacrifice. It can be all-consuming. And during that time, life may not have much balance. It's been said, "If you can't ride two horses at the same time, you should get out of the circus." A circus is not at all a bad analogy for the swirl of demands placed on leaders at the top.

Personally, I liken being a CEO to being an Olympic athlete. It's an exhaustingly grueling yet richly rewarding time when you're at the top of your game. And I ask you, when was the last time you heard an Olympic athlete complain about work-life balance?

Service . . . is the rent we pay
for the space we occupy.

MARTIN LUTHER KING
(U.S. CIVIL RIGHTS LEADER)

Thanksgiving Dinner

My mother never seemed to miss an opportunity to do a good deed as she went along her way, even when her activities became more limited in later years.

When she realized that her women's club was meeting the day before Thanksgiving one year, she mobilized her friends to help stock the community food shelf for the holiday. All committed to bring groceries to the meeting. I had volunteered to pick her up since she recently had stopped driving. Arriving late, as I often did, I found that all the other women had left. I was anxious to get my mother into the car and on the road to make my dinner engagement.

The ladies obviously had taken their call to action very seriously, as the foyer was heaped with boxes and bags of food. Suddenly the hostess realized that she didn't have a way to get the food to its destination in time for Thanksgiving dinner.

There I stood with my SUV running in the driveway.

As my mother and I drove to the food shelf, I made it "lovingly" clear that this detour in my schedule was an inconvenience, especially with a snowstorm brewing. How could it be that they hadn't planned this better?

We drove downtown in a chilly silence. As we approached the food shelf, I was shocked to see a line of people—mostly women—encircling the building in the cold. I had had no idea the need was so great.

I knew then that I wasn't late after all.

The true meaning of life
is to plant trees,
under whose shade
you do not expect to sit.

NELSON HENDERSON
(U.S. AUTHOR)

Coming Together

It's a bit outrageous to think that someone one day would decide that he is going to get together a special club and hold a meeting once a year at the foot of a mountain in Switzerland to solve the world's problems. That is how the vision has unfolded for Klaus Schwab, who created the concept of the World Economic Forum in 1971.

To recognize that our most pressing problems are too complex for any one sector of society to solve and to create a place where real work can be undertaken voluntarily by world leaders was indeed visionary. I have always credited the forum with being one of my formative leadership experiences and was honored to participate as co-chair in 2004 to help advance its mission.

Students of leadership would find a fascinating subject in Klaus Schwab. What I admire most about him is that he has never made himself the center of the forum. The participants, their thoughts, and their collaborations are paramount. For that reason, the World Economic Forum has become a model of global cooperation for all time.

Like magicians with their adroit movements, Klaus is a master at focusing all attention on the object at hand whether it be peace, social responsibility, economic vitality, or world health. He lends his vision, he attracts the audience, he sets the stage, and, most important, he lets the magic take over.

It is indeed "amazing," as Harry Truman once said, "to see what you can accomplish when you don't care who gets the credit."

In every soldier's knapsack,
there is a field marshal's baton.

Napoleon Bonaparte
(Emperor of France)

The Credo

On September 11, 2001, when the skies closed over the United States, they might as well have fallen for those who worked in the travel industry.

At Carlson Wagonlit Travel, our agents worked long, emotional hours finding accommodations for stranded travelers, facilitating baby-sitting services for parents unable to get home, even advising National Guard members on what to do when they realized their uniforms no longer fit. Our hotel employees converted one of the country's most beautiful ballrooms at the Regent Wall Street into a first responders' relief station. Our T.G.I. Friday's employees cooked and delivered food twenty-four hours a day to distraught and stranded travelers.

When we heard the news at Carlson headquarters that the World Trade Center towers had been hit, we called immediately for a phone bridge to communicate with our employees in more than 150 countries. Our instructions were simple: Take care of each other. Take care of our customers. Take care of our competitors' customers. Take care of your communities.

Finally, we told them that if we lost communication, we were authorizing them to act according to our company's credo, which requested this of them: "Whatever you do, do with integrity. Wherever you go, go as a leader. Whomever you serve, serve with caring. Whenever you dream, dream with your all, and never, ever give up."

All day long, I received reports of unspeakable horror and then corresponding acts of heroism. My heart rose and fell like a roller coaster. I had countless reasons to be proud of Carlson employees over the coming days. If only the great highs hadn't required that great plunge.

Love one another, but make not a bond
of love . . .

Give your hearts, but not into each
other's keeping.

For only the hand of Life can contain
your hearts.

And stand together yet not too near
together.

For the pillars of the temple stand apart,
And the oak tree and the cypress grow
not in each other's shadow.

KAHLIL GIBRAN
(LEBANESE POET)
FROM THE PROPHET

Love, Honor, & ?

Not too long after becoming Minneapolis police chief, Tony Bouza arrested his wife.

In the 1980s, anti–nuclear weaponry passions ran high. Erica Bouza, along with hundreds of others, had made very public their plans to stage a protest at the headquarters site of the defense contractor Honeywell, timed to disrupt the company's annual shareholders meeting.

As the story goes, Tony asked her at breakfast what she was going to do that day. She answered that she planned to protest at Honeywell. She then asked him what *he* was going to do that day. "I guess I'm going to arrest you," he replied.

That same year, I was the chair of the annual United Way campaign in Minneapolis and coincidentally found myself sharing a podium with Tony at a fund-raising event the day after the incident. His was a passionate and credible voice in describing the city's needs, but the news of the previous day was obviously on everyone's mind.

Immediately after the conclusion of his compelling speech, a member of the audience asked him how he could possibly arrest his own wife.

"She is very impressionable," he said with a wink. "I never should have taken her to see the movie *Gandhi*."

In the end, we will conserve only what we love;
We will love only what we understand;
We will understand only what we are taught.

BABA DIOUM
(SENEGALESE CONSERVATIONIST)

Pretending for Real

American Girl dolls were all the rage when my granddaughter Juliet begged me to take her to the signature store in Chicago. I was excited about the thought of spending time with her amid hundreds of life-like dolls of children from all over the world. It would give us the perfect opportunity to reflect on how rich and wonderful a diverse world can be, and we did just that.

We had tea with other little girls and their dolls from France, Sweden, and Mexico. And we later enjoyed a musical performance that underscored the universal values of honesty, kindness, and respect.

Our trip continued the next day with a visit to the Shedd Aquarium. Inscribed in stone on a wall was a quote from a Senegalese conservationist named Baba Dioum. It speaks to the importance of being intentional in teaching our children what we want society to value.

Ever since that day, while others may quote Churchill, Kennedy, and Aristotle in their speeches, I often have chosen to quote the lesser-known Baba Dioum.

I love its hopefulness. I love the fact that it gives us a path forward. I love also that it reminds me of a couple days in spring when I had my granddaughter all to myself—to play with dolls and watch the whales.

Marilyn Carlson Nelson

I, Marilyn Carlson Nelson, do solemnly swear
that I will support and defend the Constitution
of the United States against all enemies,
foreign and domestic.

That I will bear true faith and allegiance to the same.

That I take this obligation freely,
without any mental reservation or purpose of evasion;

And that I will well and faithfully discharge
the duties of the National Women's Business Council.
So help me God.

OATH ADMINISTERED BY VICE PRESIDENT CHENEY
AT WHITE HOUSE SWEARING-IN CEREMONY, 2002

Reporting for Duty

Within months after the 9/11 attack, I received a letter from the White House asking me to serve as chair of the National Women's Business Council, which advocates for women business owners with the U.S. Congress and the President.

My sense of duty ran deep, but how could I possibly do this at a time when my company was suffering so greatly? Few American businesses weren't affected, but it was a particularly paralyzing moment for the travel industry and would remain so for some time to come.

As it turned out, Madeleine Albright really made the decision for me. In a casual conversation with her at a women's leadership breakfast, I mentioned my dilemma. In a very matter-of-fact way, she recited all the "extraneous activities" she was involved in while serving as Secretary of State. Feeling somewhat sheepish, I accepted the President's invitation the next day.

I led the council for the three-year term, and, in the process, I met hundreds of accomplished and caring women business owners who inspired me with stories about their struggles for access to health care, capital, markets, and mentoring. I learned that 99 percent of *all* businesses are *small* businesses—truly the economic engine of our country. As the CEO of a multi-billion-dollar global company, I was humbled and privileged to stand with small business owners in support of all of us who have chosen business as our life work.

Looking back, I am grateful that I didn't wait to raise my hand until it was convenient. Rather, I served my country when it called—not when I could squeeze it in.

Travel is fatal to prejudice, bigotry,
and narrow-mindedness.

MARK TWAIN
(U.S. AUTHOR AND HUMORIST)

$\mathcal{A}$ $\mathcal{B}$eer, a $\mathcal{B}$rat, & the $\mathcal{KGB}$

The spirit of entrepreneurship runs deep in my family. My father often was called the "ultra-entrepreneur." So when opportunity knocks, we don't just answer the door—we fling it open wide.

In retrospect, somebody should have notified the State Department that Soviet President Mikhail Gorbachev had accepted the Governor of Minnesota's invitation to visit the state in 1990. After all, the United States and the Soviet Union had been bitter enemies for decades.

My father saw it as a great privilege to host this visionary leader at our hotel, the Radisson Plaza, and to talk about investment possibilities in the emerging Russian market. We later seized that advantage by opening the first American-managed hotel in Moscow.

When the State Department caught wind of the visit, they immediately scheduled a large advance team of security agents to scout the route of Gorbachev's itinerary. About the same time, a dozen KGB agents arrived to satisfy their concerns. The U.S. security detail could take care of themselves, but when I heard from our hotel manager that the KGB agents were getting "bored," I arranged for them to come to my home to experience a barbeque—U.S.-style—in our backyard.

They quickly went through the traditional picnic beverage: beer. I replenished it with wine. When that was exhausted, they asked through their interpreter if we had any vodka. They were very enthusiastic well into the late hours. I think they even toasted the mosquitoes.

When Gorbachev departed, his sunglass-clad KGB officers flanked him. As they somberly passed by, the last one in the group stopped. In an instant he turned to me, lowered his sunglasses, and kissed my hand. I was looking "glasnost" straight in the eye.

We are alone, absolutely alone on this chance planet;
and amid all the forms of life that surround us,
not one, excepting the dog, has made an alliance with us.

MAURICE MAETERLINCK
(BELGIAN POET)

Lika & Tutu

One late autumn afternoon at sunset, when I was particularly distraught and frightened about my son's liver transplant, I bundled myself up and went down by the lake to have a good cry. A few minutes later, I heard the pounding of running footsteps on the dock. It was our dog Lika, who leaped into my arms and pressed herself close. At that moment, I felt that we shared a heart.

Lika was extraordinarily perceptive. When my husband and I would "have words," Lika would choose sides. Standing close to one or the other, she would position herself between us as if to guard the one who most needed protection. She wasn't always on my side, and she wasn't always on Glen's side. Lika was fair-minded and, as we've reflected since, often correct in her assessment of who was right and who was wrong.

Lika died. We now have a dog named Tutu who has an obvious bias.

I try not to notice, but Tutu makes it pretty clear that she would be quite content if I were out of the picture. If I'm not there, she jumps into my seat in the car. She'll try to sit in my chair at the table. I've heard tales of her slipping into my side of the bed when I'm out of town.

Simply put, she has eyes only for Glen. It's not that I don't understand the attraction, but does she have to be so obvious with her affection?

I think so. This is, after all, the dog's gift to us: unfailing, exuberant, goofy, lovesick adoration.

Did I mention that I really miss Lika?

So when a great man dies
For years beyond our ken,
The light he leaves behind him
Lies upon the paths of men.

HENRY WADSWORTH LONGFELLOW

(U.S. POET)

The Long View

It's been said that the mark of a true leader is thinking well beyond his or her years, that is, establishing a leadership culture in an organization that becomes the organization's hallmark.

I think back to an article written for *Fortune* magazine by the business author Jim Collins, who has made a career of studying companies that last and thrive across decades. Jim was charged with identifying the "10 Greatest CEOs" of all time and the reason for their greatness.

Speaking to his methodology, he noted that he deliberately excluded some currently prominent names from the list: Microsoft's Bill Gates, GE's Jack Welch, and others like them. His rationale: Leaders cannot truly be judged until ten years have passed after their tenure.

Only then can a leader's impact be known. Did the company or organization stay the course? Did it produce other leaders who were just as successful?

When we think about the world's great leaders, did their impact not become better understood decades later? Only time made clear who was truly great.

Rather than expend all their energies on the short term, leaders who aspire to greatness beyond their time might be well advised to approach the world with this curiosity: What will generations say about them "years beyond their ken"?

I live my life in growing orbits
which move out over the things of the world.
Perhaps I can never achieve the last,
but that will be my attempt.

I am circling around God, around the ancient tower,
and I have been circling for a thousand years.
and I still don't know if I am a falcon, or a storm,
or a great song.

RAINER MARIA RILKE
(CZECH POET)

Passing the Test

Have you ever noticed what happens when two babies meet? They are absolutely fascinated with each other. I'll let you in on a secret: Business leaders are similarly intrigued with other business leaders. We note each other's styles, track the other's successes, and do a good deal of second-guessing when mistakes are made.

One leader who has fascinated me for years is Harvard Business School professor, Bill George. When my husband was vice chairman at Medtronic, I had the privilege of watching Bill's success up close while he served as Medtronic's chairman and CEO. Medtronic was a mission-driven organization, and Bill was truly an authentic leader—a powerful combination.

I remember Bill saying that he was well satisfied with his accomplishments at Medtronic but that he was discouraged that he had not had the opportunity to affect ethical corporate leadership on a larger scale. It was, after all, the era of Enron and WorldCom. Not a noble time in corporate America.

After his retirement, Bill taught at IMD, Yale, and then Harvard. He also wrote a book called *Authentic Leadership*, which he followed up with *True North*. Both prescribe a leadership model that can be born only by passing through what he describes as the "crucible that tests you to your limits."

As I sat in the back of his classroom while he taught the Harvard case study written about my leadership at Carlson, I looked at the students who surrounded me. Which ones would have the opportunity to make choices different from those made at Enron? At that moment I realized that Bill need no longer be discouraged. His legacy would far exceed his own success.

Hold your parents tenderly,
for the world will seem a strange
and lonely place when they're gone.

WILLIAM LUCE

(U.S PLAYWRIGHT)

Car Trouble

My father, Curt Carlson, was well known as a stern taskmaster, but he also had a playful sense of humor. I miss that. This is one of my favorite stories as told by longtime family friend and business author, Harvey Mackay, in my father's autobiography, *Good As Gold*:

America was holding a national election and I was hosting an election-eve party. Since it was November, the Minnesota weather gods decided to attend too, and we were socked with a nasty ice storm. Curt arrived . . . in a new Lincoln big enough to sink the iceberg that sank the *Titanic*. . . .

Then it was time to go. That is until the car-parker informed Curt that his car had slid off our ice-coated driveway, careened through a stand of trees, and wound up a total wreck on the frozen lake below. . . . Curt didn't turn a hair. He arranged a ride with a neighbor, said good night, and without a backward glance at his stricken behemoth rode calmly off in the storm.

The next day our doorbell rang and a messenger delivered an invoice for "One car, $37,432.22," accompanied by a note that read:

Dear Harvey,
No problem taking 2% off the invoice if paid within 30 days.
Nice party.
Best wishes,
Curt

Thinking to get at once
all the gold the goose could give,
he killed it and opened it
only to find—nothing.

AESOP
(FABLE WRITER C. 550 BC)

Temptation

As the clerk very carefully placed the dusty bottle of Romanee Conti in my hands, I remember thinking, "So this is the object of my husband's desire." It was the only present he wanted for his fortieth birthday. I asked him how he could proclaim it to be his favorite, never having tasted it. He said that everything he had read about the wine indicated that it was very special. And he was right, it was indeed *exquisite*.

Several years later, while traveling with another couple in Burgundy, we suggested that we take a detour to visit the vineyard where this superb nectar originated. It would be the perfect ending to the trip—a picturesque afternoon at a spectacular château overlooking the finest wine country in the world.

The small sign on a cement post was the only confirmation that the few hectares of grapevines before us was indeed the vineyard we were seeking. There was no château. There wasn't even a shed. When we asked a passerby how such a superlative product could come from this unassuming location, he shrugged. "*C'est facile. Tout est parfait.*"

He went on to explain that even in abundant years, the vintner would resist the temptation to get greedy and harvest a larger crop. Instead, he would prune back the vines reducing the yield to ensure that the wine was . . . always just perfect.

Marilyn Carlson Nelson

Trust, like the soul,
never returns once it is gone.

PUBLIUS SYRUS
(SYRIAN WRITER)

Dear Shareholders

Along with several other CEOs, I was asked to contribute to the book *Building Trust*. Here are excerpts from a personal letter I wrote to my company's shareholders—my descendants—about the covenant that binds us:

> To my children, grandchildren, nephews, nieces and family members to follow:
>
> We are emerging from a period in American business history in which obsessive desire for gain led many people to commit acts of fraud, both overt (for which some may find themselves deservedly in jail) and moral (which perhaps not technically against the law, were certainly against the common good). . . .
>
> When you are making a difficult decision, ask yourself if the decision you're about to make would show integrity, leadership, caring. And, if you make that particular decision, will you be giving up on something you should continue fighting for?
>
> These are indeed hard guidelines to follow when others around you are ignoring the rules and seem to be besting you. But know this: Their win will only be temporary. In the end, doing the right thing will always triumph. It has always been so.
>
> I urge you to always take this long view over one of expedience or convenience. This may seem like lofty and unrealistic advice, but it is what our company and our success have been built on for more than 60 years.
>
> Never forget that your role as a leader is to be a steward for future generations.

(from *Building Trust*, the Arthur A. Page Society)

There was a pause—
just long enough for
an angel to pass,
flying slowly.

RONALD FIRBANK
(BRITISH NOVELIST)

The Pause

When the Radisson Slavjanskaya opened in Moscow in 1991, it was the first American-managed hotel in the former Soviet Union and one of very few outside business partnerships. As a result of that relationship, Moscow's mayor, Yuri Luzhkov, invited me to an event to commemorate the fiftieth anniversary of the end of World War II.

As a member of the mayor's official delegation, I moved slowly through a line on one side of the Tomb of the Unknown Soldier while a queue of Russian citizens passed by on the other side. The gray skies over Moscow were a fitting backdrop for the somberness of the moment.

My heart was heavy as I placed my rose on the tomb. I was thinking in a universal way about the sacrifices of war and in a very personal way about the loss of my 19 year-old daughter under different circumstances.

As I raised my head, my eyes connected with an elderly Russian woman on the other side of the tomb. We were locked in each other's gaze for several seconds, until one of the officials from my delegation moved forward to escort me back to the entourage.

Just as I was about to step into the car, I felt a hand on my arm. It was the woman at the tomb. She was carrying a plastic drawstring bag from which she carefully pulled a small bundle wrapped in a woolen scarf. It was a picture of a young boy.

She presented it to me as if to say, "Look. This was once mine."

I gently handed it back to her. Yes, I recognize him.

If a society consisting of men and women
is content to apply progress and
education to one half of itself,
such a society is weakened by half.

KEMAL ATATURK
(PRESIDENT OF TURKEY)

Favorable Odds

People respond differently to being offered a promotion. Some are visibly elated, some feign modesty, and some can't help conveying the feeling that it's about time. But in one particular case, I was dumbfounded.

I had just offered one of the most talented women in my company a prestigious title, significantly more responsibility, and a hefty raise. She was perfect for the job, and I was pleased to be making headway in my desire to create more opportunities for women. "I am honored that you'd think of me, Marilyn," she said, "but I can't make more money than my husband. It would kill him."

I made it a point when I took the helm at Carlson to create a meritocracy. That certainly wasn't the environment during my father's era. When a group of high-performing women created a council to talk about how to make the company more welcoming to women, my father accused them of trying to start a "pink collar union." That was typical of the time. Today, Carlson's CFO, Trudy Rautio, and 40 percent of our executives are women.

I am convinced that the organizations and nations with the greatest advantage will be those which worry less about gender and more about talent. No one will be arbitrarily excluded from developing and contributing at Carlson—that includes husbands, too.

To the outside world we all grow old.
But not to brothers and sisters.
We know each other as we always were.
We know each other's hearts.
We share private family jokes.
We remember family feuds and secrets, family griefs and joys.
We live outside the touch of time.

CLARA ORTEGA
(U.S. AUTHOR)

Top Prize

My sister, Barby, was the baby, the blonde, the "cute one." Of course, now that I'm older, I never think about those things. Oh, I almost forgot . . . and homecoming queen.

When we were younger, we settled into our predictable birth order personalities. As the firstborn, I was the overachiever, the driven one, the star pupil. I practically defied gravity by being able to stay standing with the number of badges on my Girl Scout sash.

No doubt, my achievements were overshadowing at times. But as I scan the landscape of our family's challenges and determination to hold tight to one another no matter what, one figure looms large—my sister.

Barby has nurtured us all, but in particular, she gave our family countless more years to enjoy my mother as a result of her companionship. Barby delighted in taking her shopping. The only time I remember those two ever arguing was over who got to purchase the fabulous finds they discovered together.

In my mom's final years, when I so wanted to spend more time with her but was unable to do so because of my CEO schedule, Barby was there. My sister was her cherished confidante and favorite play pal. She held her hand at doctor visits and replenished her spirit as no one else could. I knew my mother was in loving hands, and for that I will always be grateful.

I guess if we're completely honest, we must admit that sibling rivalry goes on until the very end. But I readily concede here and now, there's one race in which my sister has me beat, hands down.

In moments of serious need, Barby is by your side. And in this world of competing priorities, to be there for others—isn't that the most precious gift of all that we can give to those we love?

Marilyn Carlson Nelson

In times of change the learners inherit the Earth,
while the learned find themselves beautifully equipped
to deal with a world that no longer exists.

ERIC HOFFER
(U.S. PHILOSOPHER AND AUTHOR)

Worth the Risk

"I haven't seen a movie in five years," she announced. Sharing the stage with this greatly accomplished woman who later would become the finance minister of France, I felt a bit ashamed that I actually had seen several movies during that period.

Christine Lagarde and I had been asked to talk about women in business at an event hosted by the French-American Foundation and the French Institute Alliance. At the time, she was a partner at the global law firm Baker & McKenzie. Now, as a member of President Nicolas Sarkozy's cabinet, she is working to make changes in the labor market and economic environment to ensure France's competitiveness.

I always look forward to those occasions when Christine and I find ourselves together at various events. Through these chance encounters, I learn so much. Recently she made an interesting observation.

She pointed out that while the American lexicon is filled with sayings that give people permission to try and possibly fail, this is not the case in France. "If at first you don't succeed, try, try again." "It's not whether you win or lose, it's how you play the game." "Get back on the horse and ride." These apparently have no equivalents in the French culture. It, therefore, should come as no surprise that the environment in France is quite risk-averse in regard to entrepreneurship.

I know from my own family's experience and the success stories of countless others that entrepreneurship fuels the innovation that delivers solutions, fills needs, and creates jobs. As a nation, it's a game you want to be in. In this essentially borderless era of intertwined economies and mega-markets, it seems to me that it is much riskier not to risk.

Freedom does not fall on us—freely as rain—
rather, it must be earned by each generation.

HUBERT H. HUMPHREY
(U.S. VICE PRESIDENT)

A Christmas Uprising

The grandchildren were abuzz with excitement. Outside, the snow was softly packed under the windows like great down pillows.

We were cozy, happy to be together, and pleasantly tired after a day of playing in the snow. Our family had gathered at the lodge in Wisconsin as we did every year. Christmas would soon be here.

While the holiday activity swirled around him, my son-in-law sat fixed to the television. It wasn't a football game that held his attention but a revolution happening in real time in his home country of Romania.

Marius Muresanu had come to the United States with his parents in the 1970s when it became clear that Nicolae Ceausescu was not the reformer he initially appeared to be. Brutality by the secret police was used routinely against the civilian population, food was strictly rationed, and the black market thrived. In December 1989, the people of Romania had had enough.

For several hours, Marius searched the crowd of young people battling the military in the streets to see if he recognized the faces of friends he had left behind.

When the children had been tucked into their beds, Marius said to me, "Here I sit beside the Christmas tree, in the safety of this place with my family around me, and I watched people dying in my country for their freedom. I could have been one of them. I could have died today."

It was late. He was weary. And by some luck of the draw he was safe.

The eye cannot say to the hand, "I have no need of you!"
And the hand cannot say to the feet, "I have no need of you!" . . .
If one part suffers, every part suffers with it;
if one part is honored, every part rejoices with it.

SAINT PAUL
(APOSTLE)
FROM 1 CORINTHIANS

Secret Ingredient

In today's pop business culture of motivational phrases and self-improvement books on successful management, there is no shortage of slogans about the value of teamwork: "There's no 'I' in teamwork." "TEAM: Together Everyone Achieves More." "None of us is as smart as all of us."

The fact is, they all convey what we know instinctively: Teams are powerful. Through our own experience and supporting research, we are convinced that complex problems benefit greatly from the creativity that comes from diverse thought, backgrounds, and styles. But I have yet to see a slogan that reveals the underlying secret of the very highest performing teams.

A major consulting firm figured it out. The researchers studied "successful" teams and the truly "breakthrough" teams to try to determine the differentiators between the two. They looked at the size of the team, the combination of management levels, the gender and culture mix, among many other variables.

In the end, they concluded that the greatest determinant of a breakthrough team is that the members of the team care as much about each other's success as they do about their own success.

It's well worth the investment to institutionalize a method for hiring people that's based not only on the capacity to do the job but also on the capacity to care. That is, if *you* care about more than just getting the job done.

We gain strength, and courage, and confidence
by each experience in which we really
stop to look fear in the face. . . we must do
that which we think we cannot.

ELEANOR ROOSEVELT
(U.S. FIRST LADY)

Something to Prove

The only venue we could find in 1998 to accommodate the huge turnout was the MGM Grand in Las Vegas. We had invited more than 4,000 employees, customers, partners, and family members to share with us the moment my father would turn over the reins of the company to me. Former President George H. W. Bush would speak. Wayne Newton would sing. It would be a mega-event.

As an acknowledgment of my becoming one of only a handful of female CEOs of a global company, the U.S. Air Force Thunderbirds invited me to be the first "female CEO" to fly in an F-16. My company's vice president of public relations, Doug Cody, seized on the idea and insisted that a small camera be mounted in front of me during the flight. The footage would open the event.

The idea soon lost its appeal when my Thunderbird pilot briefed me. He cheerfully delivered the news that only 20 percent of the passengers make the trip without getting sick. I determined right then and there that I had to be the one in five since all eyes were on me.

After the initial rush of the takeoff, I looked back over my shoulder at the earth shrinking behind me. "Where would we do the maneuvers?" I asked into my helmet's microphone. The pilot responded that that would happen when we were over Death Valley. "Oh, great," I thought.

We rolled and looped and did straight up and down vertical maneuvers—the only thing we hadn't done was "pull 9Gs."

I said, "Let's go for it."

Let me just say, I am grateful that I never have to experience that "thrill" again. I *wanted* to do it for my Carlson colleagues, but I felt *obliged* to do it on behalf of the female CEOs of the world. And I did do it—without retrieving the plastic bag from my flight suit.

For obvious reasons, I welcome gender parity. But there's a less obvious reason: There's just too much pressure when you're "one of a handful." It's almost enough to make you sick.

Art is the contemplation
of the world
in a state of grace.

HERMANN HESSE
(GERMAN AUTHOR)

Master Carver

Madame Chan and I communicate through a translator, but our conversations are always warmly animated with smiles, laughter, and twinkles in the eye as we talk about business, world issues, and grandchildren.

Chan Lai Wa (Madame Chan) is one of the most influential women in China and chairperson of Fu Wah International, a development partner of Carlson's. Together, we have brought Regent and Park Plaza hotels to Beijing.

But tourism and real estate aren't her family's only business successes. Madame Chan's lineage also includes skilled sandalwood artisans. Her collection of ornately carved dynastic furniture and sculpture exhibited at the Red Sandalwood Museum she founded in Beijing is considered one of the most significant collections of its kind. She was intrigued to learn that the Minneapolis Institute of Art in my hometown houses one of the world's finest collections of Asian art.

About a year after my invitation, Madame Chan came to visit. The institute's Asian art curator, Robert Jacobsen, was kind enough to take Madame Chan and her entourage personally through the galleries. He later recounted to me a moment of surprise that occurred as they were standing in front of a beautiful wooden statue of the Bodhisattva, the Buddhist deity of mercy and compassion.

Madame Chan suddenly knelt down before the image and began a Buddhist chant. Robert told me this would be somewhat unusual for a woman of her position in China who had lived through the Cultural Revolution. During that time, the government had attempted to eradicate the ancient philosophies of Confucianism, Taoism, and Buddhism. The public expression of any of those teachings has come back very slowly in China.

I don't pretend to know Madame Chan or the Buddhist philosophy well enough to fully interpret the obviously deep connection she felt in the museum. But I feel honored and comforted to know that a powerful woman from Beijing visited a museum in Minnesota and found a spiritual connection strong enough to bring her to her knees.

I am reminded that like the beautiful red sandalwood pieces exhibited in her museum, we are all shaped by a master carver.

Marilyn Carlson Nelson

I hear babies crying, I watch them grow.
They'll learn more than I'll ever know.
And I think to myself, what a wonderful world.

LOUIS ARMSTRONG
(U.S. MUSICIAN AND COMPOSER)

Special Delivery

My sister's oldest son and daughter-in-law, Geoff and Kelly Gage, were so proud to announce that they would be the parents of fraternal twins. A few years later, her middle son and his wife, Scott and Gina, announced that they were having identical twin girls.

That seemed amazing enough until we got the call that their youngest son and daughter-in-law, Rick and Britt, had just received the results of an ultrasound that showed that they were having twin boys. In case you've lost count—that's a six-pack.

Ten years after the birth of Patrick and Emma, Geoff and Kelly told them that they were preparing to adopt a baby from Russia. That decision had been inspired by a family philanthropic trip to Russian orphanages and their deep faith that another child awaited them. They were eager to receive news.

You guessed it. The natural mother gave birth to two babies. Geoff and Kelly were asked to take both. We saw this as the absolute sign that these children were meant to be in our family.

My daughter, Wendy, had two children with the help of modern medicine. True, Martin and Sadie aren't twins, but they are twin miracles nonetheless.

I sometimes reflect on my own "birthing method"—one at a time, conceived the old-fashioned way. And I am grateful beyond words for the many ways we are now able to fulfill the dreams of families who yearn for children and the dreams of children who yearn for families.

Marilyn Carlson Nelson

Tourists are very valuable to the modern world.
It's very difficult to hate people that you know.

JOHN STEINBECK
(U.S. NOVELIST)

Doing My Part

A few years ago, while attending the World Economic Forum's annual meeting in Davos, Switzerland, I received an urgent summons from a fellow attendee who was requesting a private meeting.

The message was from former Israeli Prime Minister Shimon Peres. The topic was how we could move toward a more peaceful Middle East and what part I—and my company—might play.

I had met with the prime minister once before at an aviation and travel industry dinner with former PLO leader Yasser Arafat. They were issuing a joint invitation to the world to visit Bethlehem and Jerusalem at the start of the new millennium. My role was to introduce the two leaders, who seldom shared a stage.

This time, the prime minister would introduce *me*—to his brilliant dream. "Marilyn," he said. "We will achieve peace in the Middle East, and when we do, we are counting on your industry to help keep the peace by bringing the tourism that will provide the employment and hope for young people who otherwise will be susceptible to other forces."

Then he looked at me with penetrating eyes and said, "Marilyn, it's either tourism or terrorism."

I have always felt privileged to be associated with an industry that raises living standards and provides entry-level jobs as well as lifetime careers. As the prime minister reminded me that day, its contribution is even greater. Through the continuing exposure facilitated by the tourism industry to others of different cultural, religious, and political backgrounds, there is hope that we can chip away at the hatred and prejudice that separate us. There's work to be done.

We need heroes so that
we might become heroes.

ROBERT DILENSCHNEIDER
(U.S. AUTHOR AND BUSINESS EXECUTIVE)

Looking Up

The Greeks, who had a wise saying for everything, said, "A people are known by the heroes they crown."

I believe that today we crown many heroes simply because of their good fortune, their good looks, or the fact that they've enjoyed a good season or two. We too often confuse "cool" with "courage" and in doing so incorrectly instruct our youth and even ourselves about what is important.

When I see someone being crowned a hero in the modern-day public square, I ask myself, "Is this someone I would want to host in my home? Would I want my grandchildren to sit at their feet and learn from them?"

Conversely, I see society's quiet heroes—teachers, police officers, enlistees, public servants—and mentally crown them heroes, adding my vocal and, when appropriate, financial support.

It would do us all some good to examine our own personal heroes: Why have we chosen them, and what does it say about us? Even better would be to discuss with our children and grandchildren who they have chosen as their heroes and why. From this we will better understand them and glimpse the future they will create for themselves.

I once had a sparrow alight upon my shoulder for a moment, while I was hoeing in a village garden, and I felt that I was more distinguished by that circumstance than I should have been by any epaulet I could have worn.

HENRY DAVID THOREAU
(U.S. AUTHOR)

One of a Kind

Critics of globalization sometimes point to what is known as brand homogenization as a downside to international commerce. They argue that if the world is filled with mega-brands and you can find the same products everywhere, why travel?

In general, I defend a degree of homogenization. If managed properly, companies that take their brands globally create jobs, raise standards of living, and bring consistency in the quality of goods and services, as well as enforce much-needed safety standards. As for blaming homogenization for the demise of unique products produced in a particular country, I recall my experience in Wales.

My husband and I had just enjoyed a simple ploughman's lunch in Cardiff. As we strolled along the city's cobblestone streets, we passed a store with a stunning yellow and avocado jacket and a matching plaid skirt displayed in its window. Somewhat uncharacteristically, Glen encouraged me to try it on. When I hesitated, he said that a woolen outfit would always remind me of the green hills of Wales. And when he protested at my suggestion that I buy only the jacket, I knew I had found something unique.

Back home, it was the perfect attire for a fall football party. I delighted in responding to the numerous compliments I received with the romantic story of my unusual find in a faraway place—until, that is, my sister walked in wearing the same outfit in beige and cream, which she had found in a local mall.

The mall? Okay, but did they serve a ploughman's lunch?

Leaving behind nights of terror and fear
I rise
Into a daybreak that's wondrously clear
I rise

MAYA ANGELOU
(U.S. POET)
FROM "STILL I RISE"

On the Same Day

On the same day that someone hung a noose on the office door of a black professor at Columbia University, I spent the evening with Reatha Clark King, a Columbia MBA graduate and an African-American. Reatha shared her journey from field hand to corporate executive at a gathering of business school students at the University of Minnesota. Neither of us knew about the incident that had occurred earlier that day.

Reatha talked about her decision in the 1970s to augment her PhD in chemistry with an MBA from Columbia. That decision would land her a position at the food giant General Mills and launch her into a community leadership role as president of the company's foundation. Now retired, she still wears her community leadership role elegantly, generously sharing her story and wisdom.

Listening to the news the next morning, I was chilled to the bone reflecting on our time together.

On the same day that someone prepared a noose, Reatha talked of her childhood picking cotton in Georgia, separated for a time from her mother, who had gone north to earn money to send home.

On the same day that someone transported the noose to the campus, Reatha recounted her passion for schooling, knowing that education was the only way to improve her "lot."

On the same day that someone hung the noose on the door, Reatha described the many ways we are diverse: from gender to religion to personalities. She ended by gently reminding us that "race" was the most difficult conversation our country has ever had, and she urged us not to shy away.

Yes, the talk must continue, with the hope that one day "someone" will listen.

Marilyn Carlson Nelson

What the caterpillar calls the end of the world
the master calls a butterfly.

RICHARD BACH
(U.S. AUTHOR)

Taking a Tumble

My daughter, Wendy, is full of fun and a gifted athlete—good enough at tennis to play on the pro circuit after graduating from Northwestern. At one time, she was paired with an aspiring Monica Seles. Nick Bollettieri, the girls' coach, who also coached Andre Agassi, thought that Wendy's outgoing personality would bring out the champion in the young Seles. Well, something certainly did.

Wendy was progressing so well in tennis, it's hard to fathom why she would risk it all. One year, she made the decision to break the tennis camp rules and enrolled in a downhill skiing race camp in Jackson Hole. She was emboldened by her instructor's appreciation for her athletic agility. "Perhaps skiing should have been her chosen sport rather than tennis. How impressive she'd be if only she accelerated her speed through the gates."

Rehabilitation for tearing your ACL ligament and taking a chunk out of your tibia is long. Sidelined, Wendy fell into a depression. Instead of abandoning his wayward pupil, Nick stayed with her, as he has ever since. He gave her an assignment to focus on. "Help me open a restaurant," he said. "Your family owns T.G.I. Friday's—you must have a few insights."

Wendy researched sites, requested variances from the city council, worked with the architects on the design, hired the staff, marketed the restaurant, and orchestrated the grand opening. She loved it. No longer focused on tennis, she was surprised to learn that she had inherited the dominant gene in our family—the entrepreneurial spirit—and she is now an executive in the family business.

I did love to watch Wendy move on the court. But I admire even more how she moved forward and never looked back.

Marilyn Carlson Nelson

Don't accept your dog's admiration
as conclusive evidence
that you are wonderful.

Ann Landers
(U.S. columnist)

Humility

Women MBA students are hungry to see models of female leadership—there are still so few. To address this need, I agreed to host a leadership series at the Carlson School of Management at the University of Minnesota called "Inside the Boardroom" in which I interview a female leader one-on-one and then we are joined by professors for a panel discussion.

I was fortunate to have as a guest Anne Mulcahy, one of the most lauded CEOs in American business, and for good reason. She did what several others before her had failed to do—turn around the beleaguered and iconic Xerox.

Anne was disarmingly candid during the interview, sharing thoughts and concerns that most CEOs keep to themselves. She was a refreshingly rare example of business leadership.

In her new role, there was a lot to clean up. Anne recounted the story about the day she settled the SEC lawsuit against Xerox. As a result, the company hovered on bankruptcy. She knew the settlement would make the news the next day and had braced herself for the fallout, but she never imagined the extreme effort it would take to respond to the media onslaught, bolster demoralized employees, and reassure customers and shareholders that Xerox would survive.

"At the end of this very long day," she said. "I picked up a voice mail from a former colleague who said, 'Mulcahy, you know that what you're reading in the press doesn't accurately reflect Xerox or you. That's not the real story. But here's the other piece: You'll get through this, and when you do, you'll read a story about how you turned Xerox around. Just remember, that's not the real story either.'"

Nothing you do for a child
is ever wasted.

GARRISON KEILLOR
(U.S. AUTHOR)

The Temples

As we drove through the streets of Seim Reap, Cambodia, I reached into the back pocket of the seat in front of me to track our route to the great temples of Angkor Wat. Advertisements for restaurants and hotels ringed the border of the tourist map, along with a black-and-white notice: "Sexual activity with children in Cambodia is a crime."

I was sickened and encouraged at the same time. Sex tourism involving children is a growing scourge around the world, particularly in Asia, India, and Latin America, where laws, if they exist, are not well enforced and poverty invites this type of exploitation. As I looked out the car window, suddenly every child I saw was a target and vulnerable. And there were so many children.

In 2004, I was approached by the U.S. State Department to sign on to an international code of conduct for the travel industry on behalf of our hotels and travel agencies. By signing the code, I pledged that we would educate our employees about this issue and advise our customers and partners that Carlson would take any necessary action to prevent this illicit activity. We would be the first North American–based global travel company to become a signatory.

I was counseled by several colleagues and PR experts that this was too unsavory an issue with which to be associated and that it might implicate us in a negative way in the consumer's mind. I listened, and then I traveled to the United Nations, and I signed the code.

If you haven't been to Angkor Wat, you must go. The temples are breathtaking. You'll never forget them. And now, you won't forget the children either.

In a dream
you are never eighty.

ANNE SEXTON
(U.S. POET)

In Your Dreams

I *like* speed. Downhill skiing fulfilled that desire for me until I discovered rollerblading. Like the toad in *Wind in the Willows*, I got positively wild-eyed the first time I saw someone whizzing by on that sleek modern-day version of roller skates. I determined right then that one day I would rollerblade in Central Park. It was my dream.

I wore all the protective gear and practiced at every opportunity at a park near my home until I felt confident that I had enough agility to cross streets, navigate other bladers, and dodge a mugger . . . should the need arise.

I was in my mid-sixties when my dream came true one spring day while I was on a trip to New York City. I suited up in the lobby of the hotel across from the park. It was a picture-perfect sunny day. The flowers were in bloom. The air was filled with fragrance.

Outside the hotel, it seemed like the entire city was playing hooky. I gracefully navigated the street crossing and glided onto the path. Once I realized I was in command of myself, I felt free to take in all that was around me. It was thrilling!

So thrilling that I almost forgot that I was scheduled to participate in an important conference call. As I reluctantly rounded the final turn before heading back to the hotel, I approached a park bench where an athletic-looking young man was resting. I think I probably dug in a bit more to pick up speed.

As I whooshed past him, I heard him call out, "You go, Grandma!"

Damn.

It's a little like wrestling a gorilla.
You don't quit when you're tired,
you quit when the gorilla is tired.

ROBERT STRAUSS
(U.S. PRESIDENTIAL ADVISOR)

Waiting Room Blues

Rochester, Minnesota, is an unlikely place for a center of excellence in anything other than farming. But it is here that the Mayo brothers set up a medical clinic after a tornado tore apart the community in the late 1800s. For over a century, the Mayo Clinic has served humankind from presidents and kings to CEOs and celebrities, moms and dads, children, citizens of its community, and millions of others, including yours truly. But my interest in health care started much earlier.

I'm afraid I was a rather poor "spouse's wife" at the medical conventions my surgeon husband attended. The side activities the organizers had planned so carefully for the doctors' spouses never interested me as much as the conference topics. I invariably would slip into the back of the room and later engage my husband in a barrage of follow-up questions. I didn't know then that I would be responsible for the health care of tens of thousands of people as the CEO of Carlson. And I certainly had no idea how much that responsibility would cost.

But the cost isn't my focus right now, nor is the issue of who pays for it. My concern is this—getting it right for the patient. As the head of a service company, I can't imagine being allowed to stay in business with the number of errors and the amount of dissatisfaction consumers experience with the U.S. health care system.

The Mayo brothers said early on that a "union of forces" is necessary for successful health care, and the Mayo Clinic continues to adhere to that philosophy: The needs of the patient inform the research, and the research informs the teaching, which translates to improved patient care. It's a powerful marriage of science, academics, and the clinical in which all three agree that the patient—*the customer*—is at the center.

As we work through the complexities of the health care situation or, frankly, any social challenge that seems to be entrenched, my instinct is to fall back on the philosophy of those medical pioneers and suggest that it once again will take a "union of forces" to solve the problem. That union must include the voice of the customer—you and me. And, ideally, before the next tornado strikes.

Do all the good you can,
By all the means you can,
In all the ways you can,
In all the places you can,
At all the times you can,
To all the people you can,
As long as ever you can.

JOHN WESLEY
(ANGLICAN MINISTER AND
FOUNDER OF THE METHODIST CHURCH)

In the Afterlife

"How do you plan to give back after your retirement?"

As I consider my departure from the role of CEO of a global company, I empathize completely with the indignation that Nestle's chairman and CEO, Peter Brabeck, expressed when asked this question by a reporter.

President Clinton was asked a similar question in light of his robust post presidential philanthropic activities. He was quick to respond that he would never have a larger platform for making a difference than the presidency of the United States. Peter Brabeck basically said the same thing about being the CEO of a company that is recognized for socially responsible business throughout the world. I concur.

That's not to say that after retirement we won't continue to pursue ways to contribute to the common good, but it's hard to imagine that any of us ever again will have the influence and resources we have had at our disposal to improve lives on a global scale.

I suspect that Peter counts as some of his greatest contributions his company's efforts to improve farmers' yields and the quality of crops in Latin America, the advances in water management policies he has championed to promote efficient use of water by business, and the R&D efforts the company invests in to ensure better "ecodesigns" of product packaging to eliminate waste. This story about a chocolate manufacturer gets sweeter still.

For more than 135 years, millions of people all over the world have found employment at Nestle. And ultimately, a job is the best form of philanthropy.

Perhaps they are not stars,
but rather openings in heaven
where the love of our lost ones
pours through and shines down
upon us to let us know they are happy.

INUIT PROVERB

Heavenly

Shortly after my father passed away, my five-year-old grandson, Jamie, was sitting on my lap on the airplane.

In a contemplative mood, I gazed out the window at the beautiful cumulus clouds billowing beneath us and the vivid blue sky above.

My daughter had told me that the concept of death was particularly puzzling for Jamie and that she had been struggling to explain to him the whereabouts of his recently deceased grandfather.

I commented idly to him, "Look, Jamie, how beautiful it is outside. Do you think that is what heaven looks like?"

He pressed his nose against the pane and appeared to be studying the panoramic view. Finally, he turned back to me and said, "Yes, but there would be more souls around."

Sounds right to me.

Marilyn Carlson Nelson

If you only knock long enough
and loud enough at the gate,
you are sure to wake up somebody.

HENRY WADSWORTH LONGFELLOW
(U.S. POET)

Tipping Point

There is a saying I have used often to give credit where credit is due: "It's not the final blow that breaks the rock, but all the blows that came before."

So often when success occurs, it's the one who happens to be there at the moment of triumph who gets the credit. But change is rarely that easy. It's usually due to the efforts of many, especially when it involves an institution as steeped in tradition as Harvard University.

One day at our vacation home in Wyoming, a huge bouquet of roses arrived for my daughter, Diana, a Harvard graduate. They were sent in gratitude for her giving up most of her vacation to present the findings of the first task force on women's engagement at Harvard, which she had chaired. The sender was Jeremy Knowles, dean of the school's faculty of arts and sciences.

Jeremy's contribution to creating a more inclusive academic environment was significant. In his last year as dean, 50 percent of tenure offers were made to women. It seemed progress was under way until a few years later, when Harvard's president, Larry Summers, suggested that women lack an innate ability to excel in science and engineering—a comment that sparked a firestorm of controversy that eventually contributed to his ousting.

No doubt, the sensibility that railed against this implication of a gender-based scholastic disability would not have been so keen within the Harvard community if the ground hadn't been laid years earlier by Jeremy, the task force, and countless others who over the years have championed these issues at Harvard.

Diana and I watched with great interest as the events unfolded in the aftermath of Summers's comments. Initially, it appeared that a serious detour from earlier progress was imminent until the historic moment when Drew Gilpin Faust was selected as Harvard University's first woman president. Finally the rock had cracked open.

If you're going through hell,
keep going.

WINSTON CHURCHILL
(BRITISH PRIME MINISTER)

The Prediction

When I was in my late fifties, a palm reader told me that my sixty-seventh year would be an intensely spiritual time for me. My impressionable translation of that reading: I would die at age 67. From that moment on, I marked each birthday by the number of years I had left before I turned 67 and "crossed over."

As my sixty-seventh year began, I was recovering from a hysterectomy. A few months later I was back on the operating table for an emergency appendectomy. In a backhanded sort of way, illness bestows a priceless gift, doesn't it? It reminds us of the fragile thread that tethers us. Every life has its margins.

It was also the year that I painfully let go of my dream to pass on the leadership of the family business to my son. It would be necessary to go outside the family to find my successor. I would not, after all, be the "bridge" between the generations that I had hoped would mark my leadership.

I spent a great deal of time that year praying for strength and guidance. The outpouring of support from family, friends, and even strangers was inspirational and surprisingly "knowing."

As I write this, I have thankfully just passed my sixty-eighth birthday. My prayer this year is that I never forget the warmth and generosity of the human spirit that carried me during this time.

Intensely spiritual? You bet.

Marilyn Carlson Nelson

I met a traveler from an antique land
Who said: Two vast and trunkless legs of stone
Stand in the desert. Near them on the sand,
Half sunk, a shattered visage lies, whose frown
And wrinkled lip and sneer of cold command
Tell that its sculptor well those passions read
Which yet survive, stamp'd on these lifeless things,
The hand that mock'd them and the heart that fed.
And on the pedestal these words appear:
"My name is Ozymandias, king of kings:
Look upon my works, ye mighty, and despair!"
Nothing beside remains: round the decay
Of that colossal wreck, boundless and bare,
The lone and level sands stretch far away.

PERCY SHELLEY
(BRITISH POET)
"OZYMANDIAS"

So Honored

There is a magical time in childhood—after the training wheels and before hormonal distractions—when children seem to be the most open to the world. It's a prime teaching moment. My husband and I have made it a tradition to take all our grandchildren at the age of twelve anywhere in the world they would like to visit.

Our grandson, Alexander, feeling a special name kinship with Alexander the Great, chose Egypt. Perhaps nowhere on earth is the human effort more grandly commemorated in monuments, tombs, and statues. There in the desert, we came across the gigantic stone legs of a once-powerful Egyptian ruler, its massive torso long lost to the ultimate leveler—time. It was a heroic effort to immortalize the mortal within us.

In my lifetime, I have had the opportunity to build a caring corporate culture, to fight for children's rights, promote women's equality, serve my community, and advance the tourism industry as an economic driver and platform for peace. As a result, I have been honored with numerous awards. I am grateful for each and every one and display them proudly.

In time, my contributions no doubt will be diminished, perhaps even forgotten altogether. In spite of this, perhaps *because* of this, I treasure the recognition not for the prize, for I know it will not endure, but as an affirmation that I answered the call when I could, I gave it my best, and it mattered to someone in our time together. Beyond? Only the sands of time will tell.

Marilyn Carlson Nelson

Making the decision to
have a child is momentous.
It is to decide forever
to have your heart
go wandering around
outside your body.

ELIZABETH STONE
(U.S. AUTHOR)

Mom's Favorite

As the story goes, the Maharaja of Jaipur was asked which of his dozens of children he loved the most. He replied, "The one who is away until she is home; the one who is sick until he is well; the one who is unhappy until she is happy."

All my children have taken their turn at being the one "I love the most." When I lost my daughter, Juliet, in a car accident, it seemed the ache in my heart would have no end.

Certainly, when my son, Curtis, was going through his liver transplant, he occupied my whole heart.

When my daughter, Diana, told me that she and her husband had made the decision to divorce, I understood, but my heart broke for her personal pain.

When my daughter, Wendy, shared with me the hope and despair of going through in vitro fertilization, I poured out my heart in prayer that her dream for a family would be answered.

Motherhood. It is death by a thousand cuts. It is a love that knows no bounds. And I simply can't imagine this life without it.

To each of my children, "I love you most" and never forget it.

Marilyn Carlson Nelson

To love what you do and feel that it matters—
how could anything be more fun?

KATHARINE GRAHAM
(PUBLISHER, *WASHINGTON POST*)

Gratitude

When I was a child, my favorite book was titled *The Glass Bottom Airplane*. In it, a child flew around the world in a specially equipped airplane in which the world and its people could be viewed through the floor. I thrilled at all the exotic places where the plane touched down. I truly don't know if my life has been the fulfillment of that dream or if my dream became my life fulfilled.

As I prepare to step out of my CEO role, I must confess that it feels as if a love affair is ending. Beyond my husband and children, it has given me the most rewarding opportunities to satisfy my lifelong yearnings.

To the Carlson executive team, I thank you for teaching me the boundless possibilities of "we."

To all the employees of Carlson around the world, thank you for caring for our customers and one another.

To our suppliers, thank you for enabling us to serve.

To our customers and partners, thank you for your loyalty and trust in us.

To my family, thank you for allowing me to lovingly steward our family business from one generation to the next.

To my husband, Glen, I didn't realize until I met you that *The Glass Bottom Airplane* was missing something that made it all matter—a fun and funny, brilliant and loving partner to share it.

I am convinced that it would not have mattered where my life work might have taken me. In the end, I would arrive at the same conclusion: It is all about relationships.

Year after year beheld the silent toil
That spread his lustrous coil;
Still, as the spiral grew,
He left the past year's dwelling for the new,
Stole with soft step its shining archway through,
Built up its idle door,
Stretched in his last-found home, and knew the old no more . . .

Build thee more stately mansions, O my soul,
As the swift seasons roll!
Leave thy low-vaulted past!
Let each new temple, nobler than the last,
Shut thee from heaven with a dome more vast,
Till thou at length art free,
Leaving thine outgrown shell by life's unresting sea!

OLIVER WENDELL HOLMES
(U.S. POET)
FROM "THE CHAMBERED NAUTILUS"

Coming Out of My Shell

The beauty of the tiger-striped coiled shell is reason enough to admire the chambered nautilus, but I'm also intrigued by the way in which it grows, holding tight to its center—its nucleus.

When one chamber of the shell becomes too small to house the animal, the shell elongates and widens.

The creature moves into its new home, sealing off the old chamber. It is a process of growth that will repeat itself again and again until it is finally released.

It seems to me that we, too, grow in ever-expanding circles. The challenge is always to hold tight to our nucleus—that spark of divinity that is in each one of us—all the while knowing that we will fall short of perfection, created as we are in human form.

Still I aspire, still I grow, knowing that one day my soul will slip from all constraints and I will leave behind a life marked not by the spiraled chambers of the nautilus but by my own whorled pattern of deeds done and deeds left undone, words spoken and words unspoken, time spent wisely and time wasted, love received and love returned.

Marilyn Carlson Nelson

Postscript

I am breaking format in this final section of the book, just as life sometimes does when it jogs us out of our routine with the sudden and unexpected.

"The Journey Not the Arrival Matters" is a speech my daughter, Juliet, gave before her senior class. Later that year, she was killed in an automobile accident in her first few weeks at college.

Every student in her class made a speech during that year. In a sense, it was one of many, an ordinary speech, given on an ordinary day, under ordinary circumstances. But it is not ordinary, knowing the end of the story as we do. These words from a young girl so full of love for life remind us that we have always known how the story will end; the real question is what do we do with the in-between? How do we make it count?

I give you Juliet's speech as I would share one of my most precious belongings with a trusted friend. But don't feel the need to return it; better that you pass it on.

For me, it's enough just to hear her voice again.

Do you ever feel that you are constantly getting ready for something? In the morning hurry up, rush, get ready for school . . . get ready for exams . . . practice hard . . . get ready for the game . . . get ready for college . . . get ready for work . . . get ready . . . get ready. Set goals . . . work towards them. Everything, everywhere points towards some one moment or place out there. When you are "out there" you will be happy, successful, fulfilled. Everything will be wonderful . . . there, then, when?

There's a quote from a Frenchman named Montaigne which gave me the title for my speech. "The journey not the arrival matters." Montaigne was a philosopher and a realist. He was not goal-oriented. To him it was the journey itself we should treasure. I think he was speaking of life. Life is a journey we all take, and in a sense never finish.

Let me say immediately that I am not against goals. On the contrary, they are very important milestones along the way. Nevertheless, few of us can ever be sure of our destination. I'm simply recommending that we go about our lives with a purpose. That we do not forget to value this moment today. If only we would look on today not only in the context of our journey but as an end unto itself.

Everyone in this room should live and love each day—the bad ones as well as the good. If each day we would give a friend a hug or not be so quick to judge someone we don't know and if we could all forgive just a little bit easier. Today is so valuable it should be lived and loved and enjoyed. So many of our great authors and poets have tried to tell us this.

First comes to mind Thornton Wilder in "Our Town." In the final act Emily, who has died, is allowed to come back for one day of her life. The stage manager tells her to pick an ordinary day. He knows that ordinary days are sweet and painful if you can no longer experience them. Emily picks her twelfth birthday. Emily shouts out in despair, "Mother, look at me, really look at me! Does anyone really live life every, every minute of it?"

You know, it's funny. I don't remember if I really looked at my mother this morning. I don't know when I've told her I love her. Or when I've told my friends how much they mean to me. There's always another day. Or is there?

Life is always fragile. What if . . . just what if something happened to you today? What would trouble you the most . . . an abrupt ending? Unfinished studies? Unplayed games? Unperformed dramas? No . . . I'm willing to bet it would be unsaid words, incomplete relationships and unfulfilled promises. The poet Cavafy once said:

When you start on your journey to Ithaca,
Then pray that the road is long,
Full of adventure, full of knowledge . . .
That the summer mornings are many,

That you will enter ports seen for the first time
With such pleasure, with such joy! . . .
Always keep Ithaca fixed in your mind.
To arrive there is your ultimate goal.
But do not hurry the voyage at all.
It is better to let it last for long years;
And even to anchor at the isle when you are old,
Rich with all that you have gained on the way,
Not expecting that Ithaca will offer you riches.
Ithaca has given you the beautiful voyage.
Without her you would never have taken the road.

*Each one of us is only given one journey. But if we enjoy it to the fullest . . .
every, every minute of it, one journey is enough.*

JULIET EVANS NELSON
(EXCERPTS FROM "THE JOURNEY
NOT THE ARRIVAL MATTERS," 1983)

About the Author

Marilyn Carlson Nelson is chairman and former CEO of Carlson^{SM}, a global group of companies providing travel, hotel, restaurant, and marketing services. Included in this portfolio are such brands as Radisson® and Regent® hotels and resorts, Country Inns & Suites By Carlson^{SM}, Park Inn® and Park Plaza® hotels, Carlson Wagonlit Travel®, Carlson Marketing®, and T.G.I. Friday's® restaurants. With headquarters in Minneapolis, Minnesota, Carlson-owned and franchised operations employ nearly 200,000 people in more than 150 countries and territories. In 1998, Carlson Nelson was named Carlson's CEO and chairman, succeeding her father, Curtis L. Carlson, at the helm of one of the largest privately-owned companies in the United States.

Forbes magazine regularly has selected Carlson Nelson as one of the "World's 100 Most Powerful Women." She also has been named one of "America's Best Leaders" by *U.S. News & World Report.*

Carlson Nelson serves on the World Economic Forum's International Business Council and in 2004 co-chaired the forum's annual meeting in Davos, Switzerland. She has chaired the federal advisory boards of the National Women's Business Council and the U.S. Travel and Tourism Advisory Board. She also is a member of the World Travel and Tourism Council and the Business Roundtable and is a co-founder of the Women Leaders Program of the World Economic Forum.

Carlson Nelson graduated with honors from Smith College in Northampton, Massachusetts, with a degree in international economics and a minor in theater. In 2006, she was invested in the French Légion d'Honneur for her exemplary service to humanity. She is also a member of the Royal Order of the North Star First Class, presented by the King and Queen of Sweden, and the Order of the White Rose, Officer First Class, presented by the President of Finland.

Outside her industries, Carlson Nelson serves on the boards of ExxonMobil Corporation, the Mayo Clinic Foundation, the Foreign Policy Association, and the Committee Encouraging Corporate Philanthropy and is a life director for the Minnesota Orchestra.

She lives in a suburb of Minneapolis with husband, Dr. Glen Nelson, and Tutu, their dog.